RECIPES

of My

HERITAGE

Unveiling Taste Pleasers from the Roots and Rhythms of My Ancestral Voices

Copyright © 2024 Devanni Ambalavanam RECIPIES OF MY HERITAGE

First published by Markey Writing Academy 2024

Find us on Facebook @KellyMarkeyAuthor, Instagram @Author_Kelly_Markey and LinkedIn @kellymarkey

Paperback ISBN: 978-0-6451968-8-7

E-Book ISBN: 978-0-6451968-9-4

Devanni Ambalavanam has asserted her rights under the Copyright, Designs and Patents Act 1988 to be identified as the author of this work. The information in this book is based on the author's experiences and opinions. The publisher specifically disclaims responsibility for any adverse consequences which may result from use of the information contained herein. Permission to use information has been sought by the author. Any breaches will be rectified in further editions of the book.

All rights reserved. No part of this publication may be reproduced, stored in or introduced into a retrieval system, or transmitted in any form, or by any means (electronic, mechanical, photocopying, recording or otherwise) without the prior written permission of the author. Any person who does any unauthorised act in relation to this publication may be liable to criminal prosecution and civil claims for damages. Enquiries should be made to the publisher.

Cover Design: Markey Writing Academy
Layout: Markey Writing Academy
Typesetting: Markey Writing Academy

Markey Writing Academy
Central Coast New South Wales,
Australia 2250

www.kellymarkey.com

DEDICATION

Love, appreciation and dedication to my future generation Zachary, Zara and Maila, 'Jewels in My Crown.' This is the legacy that I leave to the 'apple of my eye,' with love and honour. I pray for a beautiful, healthy planet Earth for your generation and future creation. My prayer is that you will grow up to make a tangible difference to the tapestry of our ancestors' history.

Table of Contents

REVIEWS	1
ACKNOWLEDGMENTS	5
FOREWORD	8
INTRODUCTION	10
FLAVOURS OF THE SOIL	13
ANCESTRAL PICKLES	18
FORGOTTEN VEGETABLES	24
MADUMBI OR TARO ROOT	33
HUMBLE BEGINNINGS WITH GREAT FLAVOURS	35
PROUD OF OUR ROOTS	38
ANCESTRAL COOKING OUTDOORS	41
BOMBAY DUCK	45
AUTHENTIC ANCESTRAL INDIAN DISHES	50
ANCESTRALS FOODS - OFFALS	61
ANCESTRAL MEDICINAL SPICES	63
ANCESTRAL REMEDIES	67
ANCESTRAL SWEET MEATS	76
SAVOURY DELIGHTS	79
GULGULA FILLED WITH DHAL AND FRESH COCONUT	84
LEKKER BRAAI	89
ANCESTRAL COMFORT FOODS	99

REVIEWS

Devanni Ambalavanam has shared a wealth of information in her cookbook 'Recipes of my Heritage.' This book not only depicts our traditional Indian foods but also the days in the lives of our esteemed forefathers who were shipped into Natal from Madras in South India around the 1860's, to work as indentured workers in the sugarcane plantations of KwaZulu-Natal. We indeed embrace our Heritage as South Africans of Indian origin who have managed to hold onto our ancestral roots whilst living in the apartheid era. Devanni has masterfully described the Indian culture and cuisine as this book contains specialities of snacks, curries and medicinal foods. The authentic 'bunny chow originating in Durban is a truly 'Proudly South African' Indian food. Today's culture will be pleasantly surprised by the recipes in this cookbook. Devanni has described Indian cooking with passion and creativity. She shares the Knowledge of our esteemed ancestors bringing light to their foods that are forgotten and to educate future generations. The fact that every Indian bride is given a grinding stone as a gift from her mother on her wedding day is indictive of our forefathers maintaining our rich heritage of spices culture. I have found that this cookbook has some valuable lessons on medicinal foods as well, e.g. the vegetable 'bitter gourds' has enormous health benefits in lowering high blood sugar levels in diabetics and the birth masala spice is used to treat moms who have given birth. Birth

masala is also used in the treatment of colds and flu. Masala Tea served with beautiful tea sets is a Proudly South African tradition. Devanni acknowledges our grandmothers' contribution to society. Our grandmothers were skilled in needlework, sewing and embroidery. Entertainment was enjoyed in the forms of the sari queen contest for the women and soccer and cricket for the men. These were the highlights of the Indian community. We love and honour our Indian food, culture and heritage.
Love and blessings,
Pastor Silas James. Gateway Ministries. Mpumalanga Province, South Africa.

Devanni has truly reached her goal of transporting the reader back to the ancient South African Indian kitchen. I am filled with nostalgia as I picture my own grandparents boiling peanuts and making delicious curries while reading this book. Her simple descriptions allow the reader to genuinely place themselves in colonial and apartheid South Africa through the experiences of an Indian. Her easy-to-follow recipes sound mouth-wateringly delicious and make the reader crave a good home cooked meal. In a world full of fast and unhealthy food there is nothing like a delicious meal cooked with love by a mother or grandmother. As a young millennial "Recipes of my Heritage" has renewed my appreciation for my ancestors who worked tirelessly in abusive and unfair conditions so that -hundreds of years later- I can live a privileged life. I sincerely commend Devanni on so beautifully putting across the way of life that older generations had to live and the joy that food brought into their difficult lives. This is a brilliant and easy read; I cannot wait to see what more she has in store for the future.
Vanessa Mohanlal, English Teacher.

"Coming together to share a meal is an ancient tradition of the Indian food culture, it has been carried over from generations through the years. In her book 'Recipes of my Heritage' Devanni Ambalavanam takes us back in time to the early days when our ancestors first arrived in South Africa. Our ancestors were humble and modest, leaving the countryside's of India, they sought a better life for themselves and their families welcoming the next challenging phase in their lives. With true appreciation of our indigenous roots this book aptly describes our authentic and ethnic family values and cuisine, getting together over a simple meal and making it a celebration of life. This book connects us to our ancient past and makes us appreciate where we come from. Our ancestors were promised a better life, they were promised citizenship and land but sadly this promise did not materialize, on the contrary they had to depend upon their survival skills to face each challenging day, sometimes working to the point of exhaustion and even death. Today we celebrate traditional foods in remembrance of them. We do not want to forget, we choose not to forget, we live in a country of vast diversity and we the Indian people add colour to this beautiful 'Rainbow Nation'.

Selina Redhi, Digital Marketing Specialist at SABC.

It gives me immense happiness to share my view on Devanni Ambalavanam's book 'Recipes of my Heritage.' I would like to congratulate Devanni on a true masterpiece in the compilation of her book of Recipes carried down from past generations. The book is well presented with absolute acknowledgement of our humble Forefathers. I am confident that the reader will greatly benefit from reading this book. The 'Comfort Food Recipes' are a go to when one is feeling like they need that one meal that would make them feel themselves again. The easy-to-follow recipes makes meal preparation enjoyable. Bombay duck which is not a duck but a fish was cooked outside because of the unpleasant smell and offal such as trotters, tripe and fish heads were cheap and all that our forefathers could afford. The medicinal recipes of Kings soup dhal for colds and flu and Birth Masala Spice for mothers who have just given birth shows that home remedies are in our kitchen cupboards. Cooking with the three-legged caste iron pot called the 'Bubbling Pot' was the pot our ancestors used and is famous today to make the traditional 'Potjie.' I would like to salute Devanni on this book, it will be a great addition to the recipe bookshelf.

Pastor Norman Veerapan. Grace Ministries, Florida, Johannesburg, South Africa.

Devanni Ambalavanam's book is delightfully fascinating, it brings back fond memories and tickles the taste buds. Being the first cousin of Devanni (our dads were brothers,) our families often converged at our grandparents' house in Kearsney, Stanger, in the sugarcane plantations of KwaZulu-Natal. The love and care our extended families offered us is beyond measure. It is there that we acquired the taste for traditional Indian foods that the author so lovingly presents to us. The love of growing organic vegetables was inherited from our elders. The harvesting of 'Forgotten Vegetables' from the allotment fields is part of our heritage. The method and preparation of foods was learned from our grandparents, Devanni's simple interesting recipes are sure to urge the reader to try them. Devanni does an excellent job of capturing our attention with family values that were taught by our ancestors. It is from her paternal grandma that she acquired the love for sewing, crochet and cooking. This book not only brought back fond memories but is an inspiration not only to appreciate our Heritage but to preserve our culture and cuisine.

Sarasvathy Chellan. Head of Department (English) Gauteng Department of Education.

ACKNOWLEDGMENTS

I am blessed and thankful for the 'blessing' that had my name on it, for the opportunity of writing this book 'Heritage, Roots and Recipes.' I am thankful to Kelly Markey of Markey Writing Academy for making this dream come true, this is an answer to my prayer. I am the Prize winner for an aspiring author to publish a book in 2024 kindly sponsored by Markey Writing Academy. My passion for writing with the intent of inspiring others is being manifested into reality. I am so blessed to be now part of Markey Writing Academy.

Kelly Markey, I thank you for your humility, support and for being so respectable in the process of writing this book. I thank you for your motivation and your abundance of generosity and patience. This paragraph would not be complete if I did not write about 'My Warrior Angel' a warrior on a of mission helping and empowering others, an international author of a best-selling book. Right now, I am feeling an immense amount of gratitude because I am the author of 'Recipes of my Heritage.' The pen is a mighty sword in the author's hand. I own two books written by author Kelly Markey, 'The life of Jayandra' and 'Making Sage Decisions.'

'The Life of Jayandra' is a story of how Kelly Markey lost her brother Jayandra to suicide and her journey through her grief, it brings hope to the hopeless giving us the reader tools to help others in a similar situation. Humans long for love and empathy, death cannot destroy the soul, the soul belongs to the Lord. This is has taught me to be grateful for the gift of life. Jayandra may have had limitations in his physical body, but his soul was whole. His clipped wings have grown, and he is soaring in the realm of the Spirit. He is now recognized as his story is helping multitudes of grief-stricken people that are feeling hopeless, people are fragile, and some people's grief is subtle and we

the observer should not ignore the little signs for if we are ignorant to the plight of others it could turn into a wound of irreparable damage. God knows, he has enough empathy for the soul.

'The Life of Jayandra' reminds me of the song by the singer Robbie Williams, 'Feel' where he sings in desperation, "Come and hold my hand, I want to contact the living, not sure I understand this road I've been given. And his other song "I'm loving Angels instead."

Therefore, "All the forces of darkness cannot stop what God has ordained," Isaiah 14:27

I am so glad to have contacted you Kelly Markey, I believe it was divine intervention and a divine plan and purpose for my life. I salute you! I am thankful for the fulfilment of my dreams and aspirations, I am grateful for the use of my gifts and talents on a broader platform.

I am thankful to God for all the hurdles I jumped over and made it to this point.

I am thankful to my late parents for their love and generosity and instilling great values of showing compassion and empathy towards the less fortunate and those with disabilities.

To my late husband Indrin Ambalavanam who was laid to rest on the 26 of September 2015, thank you for being the moral compass in our lives from the spiritual realms. I am thankful for Maila, my daughter Camantha's baby girl who was born on the 26 September, I am thankful to my children Odette, Camantha and Ian for believing in me, I am thankful for my beautiful grandchildren especially my seven-year-old grandson Zachary who is my biggest fan, he was sitting right next to me when I received the good news that I had won the Big Prize of becoming an aspiring author sponsored by Markey

Writing Academy, he hugged me and said, 'well done grandma!' My grandchildren make me strive to be childlike and enjoy the little pleasures in life, like Zara looking wide eyed with fascination at the hairy caterpillars crawling on the grass or when taking her for a walk we would stop to look at a bird building a nest or a spider spinning a web.

I am grateful too for the simple pleasure of talking to Maila on video chat and seeing her big smile when I say,' good morning, Maila!' for all this I am thankful. I am thankful to my family and friends for their love support, I am thankful for each well wish and each word of encouragement from my brothers, aunts, cousins, nieces and nephews and friends, I am thankful for the collective positive energy of this genuine group of individuals in my life. I am thankful for the gift of my senses, for the gift of sight, smell, hearing, taste, touch and intuition. I am thankful for healthy hands to create works of art and healthy feet to walk and exercise.

I am thankful for the comfort of the Holy Spirit, I open my heart and mind to receive every good thing instore for me, and for guarding my heart and mind from negative thoughts. I am thankful for a sound body, mind and soul otherwise I would not be able to write this book. I am thankful for fresh anointing and supernatural manifestations; I am thankful for great victories and Angels protecting me from unforeseen dangers. I am thankful to the Holy Spirit for guarding my tongue from profanity and keeping my tongue sacred for speaking truth and justice. I am thankful for my home which is 'my sacred place, my sanctuary.' I am thankful for good friendships; I pray others will seek to emulate the Christ in us. I am thankful for grace, for the restoration of my dignity and the preservation of my integrity. I am blessed to be a blessing.

"You keep in perfect peace whose mind is stayed on you because he trusts You." Isaiah 26:3

FOREWORD

As I hold this book in my hands, I'm transported back to the bustling kitchens of my ancestors, where the aroma of spices filled the air and the sound of sizzling pans echoed with centuries of culinary wisdom. It's with great joy and reverence that I introduce you to this masterpiece of South African Indian cuisine.

In these pages, you'll discover more than recipes; you'll embark on a journey through time, tracing the footsteps of generations who lovingly crafted and perfected each dish. From the vibrant streets of Durban to the tranquil shores of Cape Town, the flavours of South African Indian heritage come alive in every bite.

The inspiration for this cookbook comes from a deep-rooted connection to South African Indian heritage, a heritage that pulses with the rhythm of spices, the melody of laughter, and the warmth of familial love. Each recipe is a tribute to the resilience and creativity of our ancestors, who despite facing challenges and adversity, preserved their culinary traditions with unwavering pride.

As you explore these recipes, I encourage you to embrace the spirit of experimentation and creativity. Allow yourself to be guided by intuition and passion, just as my ancestors were when they infused each dish with their unique flair and personality.

Whether you are a seasoned cook or a novice in the kitchen, there's something here for everyone to savour and enjoy.

I extend my heartfelt gratitude to my ancestors, whose legacy continues to inspire and guide us all on this culinary journey. My hat goes out to Devanni Ambalavanam the author who has brought our ancestors legends and legacies to life in this beautifully designed book. Stella effort and thank you for passing on the mantle to future generations both in South Africa and globally. Brilliantly researched by Ambalavanam and the photograph inclusions do tell a thousand words…

May this book on 'heritage, roots and recipes' inspire the reader and serve as a celebration of South African Indian culture, a testament to the enduring power of food to connect us to our roots and unite us in shared joy of celebration. Kudos Devanni for bringing this book and heritage well and truly alive!

With love and spices,

Kelly Markey
Award Winning and Bestselling Author
Ambassador of Hope
Publisher

Kelly Markey km

CEO: Markey Writing Academy
CEO: Beacon of Hope Mission
Publisher
Writer's Consultant
Global Bestselling Author
Top Executive Award: IAOTP
Women Changing the World Finalist
Brand Ambassador:
Global Movement of Hope
Winner: Book of the Year
kellymarkey.com

INTRODUCTION

While relaxing in my garden chair looking into my garden one beautiful sunny afternoon, feelings of nostalgia flooded my mind. I fondly remembered 'forgotten foods' I had enjoyed as a child, reminiscing in the forgotten memories of my childhood of rushing home from school hungry and indulging myself in piping hot, boiled madumbis that my mom had told me she would prepare for my brothers and I to have after school or peanuts boiled in salted water, still in the shells and when the shells were opened revealed little pearls of peanuts tucked in a little bit of salted water, closing my eyes I would savour these delicacies and the moment, these were priceless memories and not forgetting the hot boiled mealies dripping with butter, all washed down with a nice cup of hot, black tea.

This gave me the idea to write this book 'Recipes of my Heritage,' simple lunches of roti and cabbage was a treat and pre-dinner snacks of chilli bites made with fiery red fresh chilli or split pea dhal fritters known as vedas to keep the hungriest person satisfied until dinner time. The silky-smooth peanut and mint chutney spread over thickly on bread was a delightful meal after school. These were memorable meals. The simplest meal would rise to the occasion like the humble vegetable biryani served with brinjal dhal and carrot salad. A steaming bowl of rasum dhal with rice on a chilly winter's evening was quite delicious, give it a try you won't be disappointed.

The memory of the cauldron, the three legged black, caste iron pot also known as the 'bubbling pot' simmering slowly on the outside fire on a relaxed Saturday evening with the weekend special of Cornish chicken curry, with soft cooking up-to-date potatoes, peas or gadra beans. Slow cooked dishes of trotters and beans, using the slow cooking method to achieve the depth of flavour, tasting better when the flavours are well integrated, with family and friends coming together the food would be finished in no time. Food brought family and friends together. The get togethers nourished their souls and sustained their bodies and uplifted their spirits.

As I pull back the curtains to reveal a period in our lives that is forgotten, I bring to you in humble reverence and remembrance the legacy of our ancestors together with a selection of delicious tried and tested traditional, authentic Indian recipes that our forefathers carried down from one generation to the next, remembering their struggles, strength, resilience and how they overcame their adversities through perseverance. I am thankful to our storytellers such as our parents, grandparents, uncles and aunts for telling us stories in our childhood and instilling in us a sense of gratitude for our Indian culture and cuisine. I have made the 'Sage Decision' that I am not going to leave out my authentic, ethnic identity as an Indian South African when writing this book. Spicy biryani with a medley of colourful vegetables or the proudly South African, mouthwatering bunny chow, the comforting taste of kitchri and tomato chutney all bring back feelings and emotions of nostalgia of days gone by. I bring to you a fusion of Ancient Indian South African recipes with exotic flavours.

Gadra beans, fresh pods of sugar beans that has not been dried
Kitchri rice and dried split peas cooked in water till it's mushy
Madumbi Yams or Taro Root
Rasum King Soup
Vedas split pea fritters
Chutney sauce

ESSENTIAL ITEMS IN THE KITCHEN

Chopping Boards – one for meat and one for vegetables
Cannisters – to hold coffee, tea, sugar, rice, beans etc
Dish Rack – drip drying of dishes the old-fashioned way
Mixing Bowl, Can Opener, Good Absorbent Dish Cloths, Dustbin, Spice Rack, Potholder, Sharp Knife, Place Mats, Ladle, Peeler

ESSENTIALS IN THE KITCHEN CUPBOARD

Brown spices – coriander powder, cumin powder, garam masala which is blend of different spices, fennel powder and cinnamon powder and birth masala powder.

Yellow powder – turmeric powder, hing also known as asafoetida
Spices - mustard seeds, cinnamon sticks, nutmeg, cardamom, black cardamom, bay leaves, cloves, fennel seeds, cumin seeds, star anise, dried mixed herbs and a good masala, I use Rombo Rossi masala as it is a very versatile masala and adds taste and flavour to any dish.

Absolute essentials in the kitchen - onions, garlic and ginger, lemons, tamarind paste, tomatoes, green chillies, fresh coriander leaves and fresh curry leaves therefore it is best to have the latter in your vegetable patch so that it is readily available. Rose water, saffron, cooking oil, butter ghee. If you need these spices, it is best to Google an Indian spice store near you and get the spices you need.

tsp is abbreviation for teaspoon, Tbsp is abbreviation for tablespoon.

1
FLAVOURS OF THE SOIL

Educating our younger generation on the importance of organic vegetables should be one of their lessons in life.

Vegetables planted in our ancestors' backyard gardens did not contain harmful pesticides or chemicals which is a norm today. Highly toxic chemicals strip the fruit and vegetables essential vitamins and minerals leaving them nutrient deficient.

This book is written to encourage the older and younger generations to explore the varieties of Indian vegetables savoured by our ancestors thus getting the full benefits from the 'forgotten vegetables.' It would help to get reacquainted with Indian vegetables, spices and herbs. It would improve our overall health and quality of life.

Spices played an important role in the diet of our ancestors, the indentured labourer. It is because of them that spices and Indian cuisine was introduced to South Africa. They planted seeds, grew their own food, preserved food, cooked their food and shared their food. They were self-sufficient because they had to be. From their early years daughters are taught to cook, presentation and palatability was of the utmost importance just as taste was. They were taught the nutritional and medicinal values of foods. They were also taught to clean house, babysit their baby brothers and sisters and learn how to make round rotis.

The pounding mortar stone and pestle was used to pound spices into fine powder and make ginger and garlic paste as well as silky smooth mint and peanut chutney.

Picture of grinding stone

Every Indian bride received a grinding stone as a gift from her mother on her wedding day. Today with modern technology life has become easy for the modern housewife. She has a wide range of appliances to choose from, today the 'Food Processor' is used to make smooth purees for sauces, this saves her time and energy.

EARLY MORNING CONVERSATIONS OF OUR GRANDMAS

"Bomi! Good morning how are you this beautiful morning?" shouted Kumari from her doorstep holding a broom in her hand. By eight o' clock in the morning her laundry was done and on the washing line and her floors swept clean, she would then glance out of her tiny cottage to catch up on the latest events that might have occurred in the community.

"Good morning, Kumari, I'm very well thanks, hope you are good this morning," said Bomi politely.

"I'm very good Bomi, what are you cooking today," asked Kumari curiously.

I'm making sugar beans curry with dried fish* and madumbi* and some boiled eggs chutney with phutu*," replied Bomi.

"That sounds very tasty Bomi, I'm making sugar cane herbs, parathas* and some mint and peanut chutney."

(Today mint/peanut chutney is like pesto, it is served on toasted bread or crackers, and it is delicious.)

Early the next morning Bomi would call out to Kumari from her doorstep.

"Kumari! You got some nice pickle; I want to have it with my sour porridge."

(Sour porridge is mealie meal in water that is fermented for a few days and cooked to make a porridge, it is an excellent probiotic for our tummies as it promotes a healthy gut.)

Dried fish* is dried snoek, snoek is also known as barracuda.

Madumbi* yams or taro root

Phutu* flaky and fluffy mealie meal porridge

Parathas* flaky flat bread

That's how our grandmothers spoke in those days, they were not highly educated, some never went to school. They were taught to cook, clean house, learn gardening, and how to be a good housewife someday.

"Yes Bomi! I'll bring you some mint and peanut chutney just now. So, she rushed into her tiny cottage and came back with an enamel bowl full of mint and peanut chutney.

"Thank you so much Kumari, you are very kind, now I'm going to enjoy this for my breakfast," she said gratefully.

These were the conversations that echoed through the compound barracks they called home on the Sugarcane Estate in the Natal

Coast. Traditional recipes passed on from grandma to her daughters and from the daughters to their daughters. They lived in harmony, expressing kindness and generosity of spirit which was the backbone.

of their culture. They would always cook a little extra just in case an unexpected visitor showed up, that is our legacy.

Today that doesn't happen much. Some of us don't know our neighbours, it's sad that those days are no more when good friendships were established. I called my long-lost friend Priscilla Lottering to ask her if I could use her koeksuster* recipe in my book 'Recipes of my Heritage.' and she willingly obliged. "Yes of course Devanni, are you going to add some of Ma's recipes on your book?" she asked. Most of the recipes in the book are Ma's recipes. Ma would never let any visitor leave without them having a meal, my friend Priscilla would always pop in for a visit and a chat and my late mom would offer her whatever it was that she had cooked. Our friendships were truly blessed, our friends mattered. Our children are all grown up now and have children of their own, but the love we have for each is still there.

We hold onto the wonderful memories of great friendships and the sentimental values we shared. We hold onto memories of visitors staying over for the night, it was a houseful of old stories and freshly baked scones and tea after a meal. Today we are thankful for WhatsApp and other social platforms where we can connect and chat with our long-lost friends and relatives, to catch up on what's happening in their lives or wish them a happy birthday, Merry Christmas or Happy New Year. My late dad always made time to visit family members. He was a man who knew how to prioritize family values, today however it's a different scenario.

Koeksuster* - syrupy doughnut

2

ANCESTRAL PICKLES

Pickles enhances a simple meal; no meal is complete without some sought of pickle. Pickles is a beneficial probiotic assisting in gut health and mealie meal soaked in water for a week is fermented and cooked to make a sour porridge. This was a favourite with our ancestors.

Our ancestors were famous for their mango pickles, cultivating and harvesting mangoes from their own backyard. They were famous for pickling green mangoes which is known as 'achar,' and who doesn't love sliced green mangoes with masala and salt.

SWEET AND SOUR PICKLE RECIPE
BY KELLY MARKEY

My mother's pickle recipe is not just a culinary delight but also a testament to the rich tapestry of her heritage. Passed down through generations from my ancestors who journeyed from North India to South Africa, it embodies the fusion of flavours and traditions that define cultural exchange. Each bite tells a story of resilience, adaptation and enduring love for preserving culinary heritage. Whether it's the vibrant spices or the meticulous preparation this recipe is a cherished link to the past, connecting you with your roots with its tangy, savoury taste. Shared with much love from my mom **Jaimathee Ramlucken, from Mandeni, South Africa.**

Recipes of My Heritage

INGREDIENTS

1 kilo green beans,

1 cauliflower, 1 bunch celery,

10 carrots,

2 turnips,

Half a kg ginger,

Half a kg garlic,

6 onions,

2 bunches radish,

2 litres white vinegar,

2 cans corn kernels,

2 bottles pickled gherkins,

2 bottles pickled cucumber,

2 bottles pickled seedless olives,

1 seedless prunes,

1 kg raisins,

3 small bottles granulated mustard,

2 large tins pineapple pieces,

1 litre cooking oil,

1 kg Packo pickle masala,

1 Tbsp chilli powder, salt,

anchovies (optional.)

Clean vegetables and chop finely. Cut cauliflower florets into small pieces. Clean, peel, rinse carrots and turnips and grate. Place in boiling water for 10 minutes and strain water. Boil 2 litres of white vinegar and put the veggies into it, close and let it soak for 5 days and thereafter strain off half the quantity of vinegar. Drain and discard the liquid of 2 cans of corn kernels and add. Drain the pickle juice of the 2 bottles of pickled cucumbers, 2 bottles of pickled olives and 2 bottles gherkins and store in a jar with a lid and keep in the refrigerator,

I have a wonderful tip for you using the pickle juice*.

Add 1 kg prunes, 2 large tins pineapple pieces, drain the juice of the pineapples into a container with lid and store in refrigerator for later use, 1 kg raisins, 3 small bottles of granulated mustard, add diced anchovies. Cut up all the above-mentioned pickled items into small pieces. Warm up 1 litre of cooking oil and add in 1 kg pickle masala, (South African Pickle Masala,) if available. Some pickle masalas contain salt so be cautious with the salt. Packo Pickle Masala does not have salt in it. 1 Tbsp mixed chilli powder, South African product if available. Add salt to suit your taste buds.

Stir for 5 minutes and pour into the veggie pot. Keep mixing every few hours and leave closed for 5 days. Add the juices from canned pineapples, using this instead of sugar. Add the 3 small bottles of granulated mustard and chopped anchovies and mix well. Transfer into storage jars. The quantity can be scaled down be halving the ingredients. Enjoy this sweet and sour delight.

Mixed vegetable pickle is a common accompaniment to any meal often made with whatever vegetable available during the season such as cauliflower florets, carrots, green beans, green chillies, or cabbage preserved in the amber liquid of a mix of mustard and sunflower oil and pickle masala. Slow roasted to perfection and ground with a mortar and pestle, pickle masala adds depth in flavour to the pickles. Pickle masala is made up of spices such as crushed cumin, coriander fenugreek and chilli flakes. Tangy to the tastebud's pickles provide a gastronomical experience to the person savouring it for the first time.

DIP FOR SLICED GREEN MANGOES

1 Tbsp sugar

1 tsp salt

1 Tbsp masala

Juice of 1 lemon

2 Tbsp vinegar

Mix all ingredients well This is the dip for sliced green mangoes.

TIP

Pickle juice - use pickle juice to make vegan cheese. Puree 250 g cashew nuts in a blender adding tablespoons of pickle juice at a time to make a thick paste and voila you have vegan cheese. Be careful not to add all the pickle juice at the same time but one tablespoon at a time until you have the right consistency. Enjoy!

VEGETABLE PICKLE
BY VILO NAIDOO

Mixed vegetable pickle is a common accompaniment to any meal often made with whatever vegetable available during the season such as cauliflower florets, carrots, green beans, green chillies, or cabbage preserved in the amber liquid of a mix of mustard and sunflower oil and pickle masala. Slow roasted to perfection and ground with a mortar and pestle, pickle masala adds depth in flavour to the pickles. Pickle masala is made up of spices such as crushed cumin, coriander fenugreek and chilli flakes. Tangy to the tastebud's pickles provide a gastronomical experience to the person savouring it for the first time.

Vilo Naidoo and I were in the same class in High School, one of our subjects in school was 'Cookery.' This vegetable pickle recipe is Vilo's speciality, she sells her pickles in jars and her happy customers always come back for more. This vegetable pickle recipe a small quantity for a couple or a small family.

INGREDIENTS

8 carrots, cleaned and diced

10 green beans chopped into small pieces

1 cauliflower chopped into small florets

SPICES

2 Tbsp chilli powder

4 Tbsp pickle masala

Half a tsp coriander seeds

Half a tsp cumin seeds

Half a tsp fenugreek seeds

Half a tsp fennel seeds

Few cloves of garlic (optional)

Half a cup sugar

1 Tbsp salt

1 cup vinegar

4 Tbsp sugar

One and a half cups oil (sunflower oil)

METHOD

Wash and dry vegetables in a clean, dry dish cloth. Once dry add in half a cup of sugar and 1 Tbsp salt. Leave to soak overnight. Drain the next day. Boil 1 cup vinegar. Add 4 Tbsp sugar, mix well until sugar dissolves. Add 1 and a half cups oil, boil further for a further two minutes, leave one side to cool. Place vegetables in a mixing bowl, add 2 Tbsp chilli powder, lightly crush these seeds in a pestle and mortar or a coffee grinder before adding to the vegetable mix. Add in the cooled oil and vinegar mixture and mix well. Taste to check if the salt is right. Garlic cloves can be added to your vegetable pickle and mix well.

TIP

1 cup bor.[1], figs or dried fruit

Half a cup vinegar

2 Tbsp sugar

METHOD

Boil vinegar and sugar, wash bor, figs or fruit thoroughly and fry and add to boiled vinegar and sugar mix, mix well and add to vegetable pickle. Enjoy!

From the authentic biryani dish to traditional curries, split pea soup or dhal curry, soji[2] a sweet dessert made from semolina these dishes represent me and my culture as an Indian. Dhal curry was cooked everyday by our ancestors to go with and pickles, sometimes with vegetables, fried fish or poultry depending on the availability of the latter.

---

[1] Bor - small dried fruit with a hard seed inside
[2] Soji - semolina pudding

3

FORGOTTEN VEGETABLES

Forgotten Indian Vegetables

Forgotten vegetables are vegetables that our millennials those born between 1981 to 1996 are less likely to buy at a greengrocer, some may eat forgotten vegetables if their moms prepare it for them. Generation Z those born between 1997 to 2012 onwards may never even heard of forgotten vegetables or may have not acquired the taste for forgotten vegetables.

What are forgotten vegetables? These are bitter gourds, okra, loofah, green banana, moringa, jackfruit, madumbi also known as yam or taro root. These vegetables were popular with our ancestors, with their harmony of flavours and textures, incorporating these vegetables into our diet has enormous health benefits. The texture of the bitter gourds resembles a crocodile, this vegetable is beneficial in lowering blood sugar. Humble dishes were never boring, green jackfruit cleaned and cut into wedges can be dipped in spicy batter and fried, green banana peeled and sliced in half can also be prepared this way. Our ancestors would take the humble taro root or madumbi which is usually boiled in salted water and turn it into a mouthwatering curry adding curry leaves and a hint of tamarind to make a tangy sauce.

I fondly remember visiting my granny Tilly on the sugarcane estate where she lived during the school holidays and eating 'forgotten vegetables' there. There was once a bowl of bitter gourd curry on her kitchen table. I was hungry and tasted it, I was ten years old and it tasted awful, I had not acquired the taste for this vegetable yet. This curry was bitter, so I threw the curry into the dust bin in disgust. My granny later looked for her curry and I told her that I threw away the bitter gourd curry. My granny was not too happy and gave me a scolding. I even complained to my mom that granny always cooked brinjals, however today brinjal is one of my favourite vegetables. Today we cherish the memories of our late parents and grandparents, God bless their souls. Times have changed.

Granny sold steamed rice cakes called 'idli' she sold idli for five cents each, it was delicious and 'sold like hot cakes.' It was a sweet cake made from ground rice flour that she made herself by pounding the rice in a pestle and mortar and sifting it, she would then add in desiccated coconut, sugar, vanilla essence, baking powder and different colours of food colouring to different batches to make different colours of idli. She even sold samosas. She would make meat mince for the samosas when she had run out of meat mince. She would chop up the meat into fine pieces on a chopping board. She also made her own samosa strips. Today we buy the samosa strips readymade and convenient to use at the grocery store. Granny could crochet and sew; she was a dressmaker. I remember the black and white poncho she made for me after she had seen it in a movie.

I often reminisce on those days when I went to my grandmas for the school holidays on the sugarcane estate. People were kind, friendly, always hospitable with big beautiful hearts. Those days when a friendly wave of the hand was accompanied by a smile as a gesture of greeting. Today I try to recreate a loving and caring environment for my grandchildren. I visit unannounced taking them special treats. It's heartwarming to see the surprised look on Zach and Zara's face when I call out, 'surprise!' I would then make myself a cup of tea and enjoy their company. Sometimes Zara would want me to read her a story. She would say, "stowy pweez gwanma." I don't see Maila often as she lives in another city but her mom does bring her over to visit and spend a few days at grandma's.

In today's busy, modern world of technology many strive to make the time to be around those they love. So much has changed in our lifetime. I am grateful that all is not lost. Here we are still gracious and loving and being there for one another passing down our family values, uplifting one another and sharing recipes. I am grateful I have my daughter Odette close by and my daughter Camantha visiting me from another city with her seven-month-old daughter Maila to spend Mother's Day with me. Those are precious memories safely hidden in my heart and memory closet. I am grateful for my blessings.

I recall the day when my husband Indrin passed away nine years ago and I had to call family and friends to give them the sad news, all I heard was, "I'll be right over," and they turned up from near and far, some of them driving six hundred kilometres to be with us. They would come with their families, wholeheartedly helping with the funeral arrangements and cooking meals for all the people that had come to pay their respects. Just their genuine, comforting presence was enough to get you through those sad moments.

ANCESTRAL CULINARY ROOTS

Our ancestors would later become much sought after cooks for their excellent culinary skills and their knowledge of herbs and spices. Their employers relished the meals prepared by them especially game dishes. The exotic aromas of fried onion, ginger and garlic paste, sliced green chilli, curry leaves in ghee would fill the air sending an eager anticipation towards mealtime.

ANCESTRAL ROOTS AND RHYTHMS

English is my first language, my parents spoke English to us, English was the first language at the school I attended. My paternal grandfather spoke English, he worked as a cook for the owner of a huge sugarcane plantation from the 1920's. Books and novels were handed down to my grandfather by his employer, who gave them to my dad and my dad passed them over to me. I distinctively remember two books that had an impact on me, one was on etiquette and the other my favourite, the life of Anna Pavlova the famous Russian ballerina. Today there's a famous dessert named after Anna Pavlova called 'Pavlova' a meringue dessert that's crispy on the outside and soft and chewy on the inside and melts in the mouth, topped with juicy red ripe strawberries.

I was thoroughly intrigued reading the book on etiquette, the book teaches one how to eat certain foods such as oysters and caviar and how your soup bowl should tilt away from you and not towards you, which fork is used for fish and which spoon is used for the dessert, I however was grossed out with the idea of eating a slimy oyster just opened, still alive with a bit of sea water in it, a squeeze of lemon juice and tilting that into my mouth and savouring the taste of the sea or eating raw fish eggs on toast or crackers, fish eggs from the sturgeon fish found in the seas of Norway. I do not know which is worse the raw oysters or the raw fish eggs.

These books impacted me greatly at an impressionable young age. My love for ballet and the opera came from reading the life of Anna Pavlova the world-famous Russian ballerina famous for the ballet 'swan lake.' I thoroughly enjoy musicals as well; I embrace this period of lifestyle and culture as part of my growth and learning period.

When our ancestors came to South Africa in 1860's they had to adapt to a new lifestyle and a new language as that would make it easier to communicate with their employers otherwise, they would have been miserable and lost in translation hence English becoming our first language. Our forefathers had special names for each other, this was a brand name according to your job description, 'Terms of Endearment' such as tractor Marie, painter Marie and the women would be called dressmaker aunty, mithai amma, nuts and sweets aunty or news reporter aunty. My dad was known as mechanic uncle.

My grandparents were second generation Indian South Africans.

Picture of my grandparents

I never saw my grandmother she passed away before I was born. My dad told me stories of her walking to the market and not taking a bus so that she could save the bus fare to buy food, she never owned shoes it was probably by choice or preference. I do not have memories of my grandfather either, he passed away when I was three years old. My older cousins would tell the younger cousins' stories of their fond memories of him. He would take them juicy, ripe mandarins when he visited them that he had plucked from the orchard he had planted in his backyard. He would tuck a dozen of these mandarins into the huge pockets on the inside of his huge, long coat that he wore, and they would eagerly await his visits and run to greet him and welcome him.

I have fond memories of the rose garden with fragrant English roses on the farmhouse property my grandparents lived in and later my dad's older brother and his family in the sugarcane plantation. There was a huge mulberry tree that I enjoyed plucking ripe mulberries from, at times staining my clothes and getting a scolding from my mom for staining my clothes.

ANCESTORS ARRIVAL TO SOUTH AFRICA

Arrival of Indians to South Africa in 1860

Upon arrival in their new home our ancestors were given worn out shacks to live in. They started the backbreaking work of digging up the soil and planting the sugarcane. Planting conditions were harsh, they harvested the sugarcane, placed the sugarcane on top of their heads and took the sugarcane to the mill by foot to get it processed into sugar. They were treated as common peasants.

Their toilets were outside and going to the loo at night was a dangerous mission, there was the possibility of stepping on an unsuspecting snake and getting bitten and of course mosquitos which were plentiful, so they used old paint buckets which they kept inside the shack to use as a loo* at night. This made it easier for children, pregnant women, women who had just given birth and for the elderly grandparents.

Loo* - toilet

DESTITUTE WORKERS ENSLAVED BY DEBT

Indian Workers Enslaved by Debt

With meagre wages life was a constant struggle for our forefathers. They planted and cultivated fruit and vegetables and would wait patiently for harvest time to enjoy the fruit of their labour, if there was extra, they would share with those in need. They had to supplement their diet in times of scarcity while waiting for their crops to be ready for harvest, in these trying times they would go foraging for wild mushrooms, dandelion greens and weeds called umfino*. Today the closest taste to wild mushrooms is oyster mushrooms or porta bellini mushrooms. There was an abundance of watercress in the rivers and streams which they relished.

Umfino* - wild greens or weeds that are edible and nutritious.

HUNTING AND FISHING

They would hunt rabbits and guinea fowl, fish in rivers, streams and the ocean, the men would leave home for the beach while it was still dark, while everyone was sound asleep, carrying their fishing rods, worms that they had dug up to use as bait and a lantern to illuminate the pathway. They would walk for miles hoping and praying that they would catch fish. They would have to return before sunrise to go to work in the sugarcane plantation. Flying termites was in abundance after a thunderstorm, the termites would be collected and fried with rice and eaten as a meal or a tasty snack.

With little money life was hard for our ancestors, they had families to feed. Mothers worked alongside the fathers; children worked alongside their parents, the very young children had to babysit and take care of the babies. They worked from sunrise to sunset in any weather condition, if they worked fewer hours, it meant lesser wages. In the little time they had off work which was a Sunday they tended to their vegetable gardens and sowed their precious seeds. Yams or madumbi was planted alongside the riverbanks where the soil was usually rich, and water was easily accessible. Rainwater was harvested and stored in drums for drinking and cooking.

4

MADUMBI OR TARO ROOT

Eating madumbis is an acquired taste. Madumbis are highly nutritious and can be eaten after it has been boiled in salted water until its tender. Madumbis support our health and prevents certain diseases, it is a versatile vegetable and can be added to other dishes as a thickening agent. Sugar beans and mix vegetable curry get a thicker gravy when madumbis are added to it. These root vegetables are a good source of manganese, potassium, vitamin B6, vitamin E and copper as well as a high source of fibre supporting a healthy gut. Boiled madumbis can be eaten with a hot sauce, coriander sauce or fruit chutney. Fruit chutney is a blend of dried apricots, chillies and spices. Our ancestors enjoyed boiled madumbis with vinegar chillies that they preserved in jars, vegetables such as carrots and pickling onions was added to the vinegar chilli jar with some salt, these preserves were enjoyed with their meals.

INGREDIENTS

Half a kg of madumbis

4 Tbsp of cooking oil

1 small onion thinly sliced

1 sprig curry leaf, rinse and remove stalk

2 green chillies sliced in half

Half a teaspoon tamarind concentrate

1 small tomato grated

Half a teaspoon of cumin

Half a teaspoon mustard seed

1 tsp salt

2 Tbsp of Rombo Rossi masala

METHOD

In a pot sauté onions, curry leaves, chillies, cumin and mustard seeds until onions are golden in colour. Add masala and stir, then add in drained madumbis, salt and half a cup of water and stir. Close the pot and let it cook until madumbis are tender, add a little water at a time the consistency of your choice, now add in grated tomato and tamarind paste and cook for three minutes thereafter stir and garnish with coriander leaves, serve with rice or rotis, enjoy!

TIP FOR PEELING MADUMBI

Caution when cleaning, slicing and rinsing madumbis, please wear gloves, as it may cause intense itchiness and irritation which is not pleasant and takes a while to be relieved.

TIP FOR MASALA USAGE

I use Rombo Rossi masala for all my vegetable dishes, it is suitable for vegetarian dishes, I am vegetarian. Please use a masala of your preference. Masala is a blend of chilli powders and spices. Kashmiri masala, Bombay Delight and Osman's Taj Mahal are a wide range of masalas available here in South Africa. These masalas are suitable for meat and vegetable dishes. The only way you will know is by trying it to see which one you like best.

5

HUMBLE BEGINNINGS WITH GREAT FLAVOURS

Culinary delights from our ancestors

Our ancestors loved to eat boiled peanuts. They planted, harvested and enjoyed boiled peanuts with a hot cup of tea. Our ancestors' humble beginnings on arriving to the South African shores from India over one hundred and sixty years ago was not on a comfortable ship. They were cramped and huddled together as indentured labourers to work in the overseas colonies and shipped around the world to different countries such as Mauritius and the Caribbean islands. They envisioned leaving India for their new jobs as an opportunity to become prosperous. This is what the Indian government told them. They did not prepare for any hardships that they might endure. They signed contracts with their employers which was an agreement and boarded a ship from India. It was an agreement between them and their employer that they would work for a particular number of years and as soon as they signed that contract our ancestors lost their freedom and so they were shipped around the world for the period of their contract. Most would never return to India, they were bought, sold, overworked in similar ways to slavery. The journey from India was arduous and life on board the ship was difficult. Heart wrenching stories of them being mistreated was told by many storytellers and historians. They were humiliated because they were uneducated, young women were at risk of being molested or raped.

They clung to their dreams and prospects of a better life for themselves and their children in a strange land thus embarking on this perilous journey. They faced many challenges, the journey was long, uncomfortable, cold and dreary. Families held onto each other on the deck of the ship, holding onto their meagre belongings which included spices, precious vegetable seeds and seedlings many of were medicinal plants of moringa, ginger and garlic, lemon, chilli, tamarind, bitter gourds, snake gourds, loofah, mangoes, bananas, coriander, mint, curry leaves, shallots and butter ghee (clarified butter.)

Chopped shallots sautéed in butter ghee with green chillies sliced in half, curry leaves, cumin and mustard seeds greatly enhanced the flavour of the butter ghee thus adding flavour to any dish. This formed the base of any curry or biryani. Our forefathers prepared the simplest meals with meticulous care, they would forage the fields for wild mushrooms and field herbs known as umfino.[3], they called the field herbs, 'sugarcane herbs.'

Sugarcane herbs grew in abundance in the sugarcane plantations of Natal now known as KwaZulu Natal. They would enjoy this wild herb dish with rice and dhal or prepare a flat bread called naan or rotis which is unleavened Indian bread also known as chapati.

Our ancestors' roots go back to the Agrarian society deeply entrenched in cultivating fruit, vegetables and flowers.

There was no etiquette when partaking of the meals prepared, no forks, knives, spoons or plates were used, just the simplicity of using their fingers to eat their food. Their plates were banana leaves. Food eaten on a banana leaf was a custom that originated in South India, now it has been scientifically proven that food eaten on a banana leaf makes you healthier. Banana leaves have antibacterial properties which kills germs when food is placed on it. Banana leaves add flavour to the food as it has a wax coating, the wax melts when hot food is placed on it and gives flavour to the food. Banana leaves are ecofriendly, biodegradable and a hygienic way of eating. It is a good practice nowadays to use banana leaves instead of aluminium foil or plastic cling wrap. Banana leaves help heal wounds, relieves pain and inflammation.

---

[3] Umfino* - wild greens and weeds that are edible and nutritious

6
PROUD OF OUR ROOTS

India was a thriving, vibrant industrial nation for centuries. India was famed for her fine textiles of cotton and silk and her precious stones of rubies and gemstones, the 'Kohinor Diamond' one of the largest diamonds in the world was found in India. The British landed there and took the diamond and other resources and left India drained and suffocating and the peasants dying of starvation. Mahatama Gandhi led a peaceful resistant movement to free India from the British rule. Mahatama means 'Great Soul.'

Our ancestors had high expectations when they chose to embark on this journey to their new land. The ship was crowded but they did not mind for they all had the same hopes and dreams of a better life, even for the stowaway Indian Myna bird that accompanied them. In the distance the thunder rumbled. They were going to work in the 'sugarcane industry.' Life was a struggle in India, in South Africa they were promised land and citizenship but sadly that promise was never fulfilled.

Many came from the rural countryside's of India and many were low caste Indians, the rejects of society, pariahs who never fully understood what they were getting into, they just wanted to get out of the place that dehumanized and belittled them not knowing that a similar fate awaited them in their new home. They were quickly disillusioned when many died on board due to sickness and disease caused by overcrowding and poor sanitation. With tears welling in their eyes many shook their heads in disbelief. The atmosphere was tense, thick and dreary as their desperate and frightened sobbing echoed through the cabins at night. They had watched many die and thrown overboard, they had not signed up for this but there was no turning back now, they would have to endure this arduous journey for a better life was awaiting them.

DRIED SPLIT PEA SOUP WITH CLOVER LEAVES ALSO KNOWN AS SOUR DHAL

INGREDIENTS

1 bunch of clover or one cup of leaves rinsed

1 cup dried split peas

1 cup water

1 tsp salt,

Quarter tsp asafoetida, spice that prevents flatulence

4 Tbsp coconut oil or a cooking oil of your choice

1 small onion thinly sliced

4 cloves garlic, slivered

3 dried chillies

1 tsp turmeric powder

1 small tomato grated

Half a tsp cumin seeds

Half a tsp mustard seed

Half a tsp tamarind concentrates

METHOD

Rinse dried split peas (dhal) and cook with 1 tsp salt and asafoetida until soft and mushy, keep aside. Heat oil in a soup pot on medium heat, add onion and sauté until it is translucent, add slivered garlic, red dried chillies, cumin/mustard seeds and turmeric powder. By now your kitchen should be smelling fragrantly aromatic, once the garlic has turned golden in colour add clover leaves. Cook for three minutes by now the leaves have wilted and reduced in size, add grated tomato and cook for a further minute or two thereafter add tamarind paste and cooked split peas, cook for a further ten minutes until all ingredients are well combined. Add water to the consistency you would like. Serve with buttered toast or rice.

TIP

For best results it is better to boil dried split peas together with a cup of water, salt and asafoetida in a pressure pot.

7

ANCESTRAL COOKING OUTDOORS

Cooking outdoors was a cooking method passed down to us by our ancestors. There is no doubt that meals cooked over an open wood fire is delicious. This was the way our ancestors cooked as indentured labourers in South Africa. They would go to the river to do their laundry and fetch water for drinking and cooking and if the weather were favourable, they would bathe in the river using the dried inside of the loofah squash which made an incredible scouring sponge to scrub themselves. Drinking water was always boiled first before drinking, this was the safe way to drink river water.

SNOEK (BARRACUDA) BRAAIED OVER COALS

South Africa's favourite fish on the West Coast, popular in Cape Town. Today fresh snoek also known a barracuda is enjoyed when braaied over hot coals.

INGREDIENTS

1 whole snoek cleaned and rinsed

2 tsp salt

2 Tbsp garlic paste

1 tsp masala or more

Few slices of lemon

2 green chillies sliced in half

Fresh coriander

3 Tbsp Mrs Balls Chutney or similar chutney

METHOD

Carefully marinate snoek with salt, garlic paste, a hint of masala, a few slices of lemon, slices of green chilli, fresh coriander leaves and Mrs Balls chutney, a chutney made from apricots, chilli, onion and spices. The marinated snoek is then wrapped in baking paper and then tin foil and placed on the braai stand of hot coals.

TIPS

NETTING SHRIMPS AND OTHER RIVER DELICACIES PASSED DOWN FROM GENERATION TO GENERATION

At the river our ancestors would tie a piece of chicken skin to a fishing line and use this to catch fish and crabs, they would dig for cracker shrimps on the sides of the river or use nets to catch shoals of shrimp. While at the river they would make an outdoor fire, clean their catch and place it in tin cans and cook it in water, fish was cooked over the open fire. They would eat this meal of fish, crabs and shrimp on the banks of the river. They would bring some uncooked shrimp home salt it, dry it and store it in jars, this was used to enhance the flavour of vegetable dishes.

COOKING FISH

Another favourite method of cooking fish was by marinating the fish with salt, spices, garlic paste, some ghee to prevent the fish from becoming to dry out. The fish was then carefully wrapped in layers of banana leaves with string called twine. They would then dig a hole about half a metre deep, lay a few stones and lay the fish over this, cover the hole with soil, pressing the soil lightly. They would then place hot coals over the soil gradually and cooking the fish for an hour and enjoy this with dhal and rice.

INGREDIENTS - FISH CAKES

500g hake cooked and flaked

2 potatoes cooked and mashed

2 onions chopped

2 green chillies finely chopped

Half a cup of finely chopped shallots

Half a cup of finely chopped herbs such as dill, coriander and parsley

1 tsp cumin seeds

1 Tbsp salt

1 egg

half a cup dried breadcrumbs plus more for coating

METHOD

Mix all ingredients together in breadcrumbs and fry. If you are using an air fryer add in 60 ml oil to the mixture and air fry for 10 to 15 minutes depending on how crispy you want the fish cakes.

TIPS

Place fishcakes onto air fryer paper, it keeps the air fryer crumb free.

MUST DO

A highlight of visiting Cape Town for a visitor is taking your time and savouring a meal of fish and chips whilst enjoying the view of Table Mountain, a world heritage site. The fishing villages in Cape Town boast of many fish and chips spots where one can enjoy snoek.

TIP FOR STAIN REMOVAL

Our ancestors loved a delicious fish curry or tasty crab dish however the curry sometimes dripped onto their clothes causing it to stain. Our ancestors would use one brand of soap to remove the stains from their clothes and that soap was 'sunlight soap' a green bar of soap that was excellent in removing stains from clothes, oil stains on clothes can be removed by rubbing sunlight soap over the stain, allowing it to rest for a while and washing it by giving it a little rub. Today we still carry on the tradition of using sunlight soap to remove stains from clothes and leaving it out in the sun to dry.

Our ancestors used only one brand of soap to do their laundry, wash their utensils and bathe with and that was 'sunlight soap.' Another tip of removing curry stains from your clothes is by sprinkling talcum powder over it, the powder will absorb the stain and with a little scrub with a little detergent the stain will be out in no time.

8

BOMBAY DUCK

Bombay Duck

A favourite with our ancestors, Bombay duck has an interesting history behind the fish name. During their occupation of India, the British loved this fish and called it Bombay duck. As the British headquarters was at Calcutta, the British officials would relish this exotic fish, the fish was transported from Bombay to Calcutta by mail train called the 'Daak' in Hindi. The local Indians of Calcutta called this fish 'Bombay Daak fish.' The British also recognized the fish with the same name but pronounced or misunderstood Daak as duck and that is how Bombay Daak became known as Bombay duck.

Sad stories of how our forefathers were mistreated and even beaten to the point of death. A picture can tell a story, a picture can paint a thousand words. Many were the atrocities carried out upon our forefathers by their employers. Our indentured forefathers continued to work on the sugarcane plantations long after indenture ended in Natal in 1911.

There's a sad story of an indentured labourer dying from food poisoning often told to us children by my late mom, when we were fussy at mealtimes. The indentured labourer wanted save enough money so that he could go back to India. He bought a bag of mealie meal and a piece of dried snoek. He tied the snoek with a piece of string and let it hang near the fireplace, he would make himself a meal of plain mealie meal porridge, he would look at the snoek while having his porridge. He eventually saved enough money to go back to India, he made himself a meal of mealie meal porridge and this time he was going to have it with the dried snoek that was hanging near the fireplace. Unfortunately for this poor indentured labourer he died after having his last meal. The cause of his death was the dried snoek, it was covered in soot.

ANCESTRAL RHYTHMS OF A SATURDAY EVENING

On Sundays, our ancestors got the day off. Saturday evenings they would gather around an open fire and socialize sharing in conversations and homemade concoctions of pineapple, ginger or sugarcane juice, lemonade was a favourite drink savoured by our ancestors, mango juice was also a traditional Indian beverage. Their get togethers helped them forget all their hardships and worries. They raised chickens and ducks and on Saturday evening a tasty chicken curry was prepared. The chicken was slaughtered and steeped into boiling water this made it easy for the feathers to removed, the cleaned chicken was the seared over open flames to burn of the fine feather and causes the skin of the chicken to cling to the flesh so that it does not fall apart in the cooking process. The down feathers were washed, dried and used as stuffing for pillows.

Special side dishes would be prepared as a pre-dinner snack. The side dishes consisted of giblets the liver, heart, chicken skin, chicken heads, gizzards, intestines cleaned well and the small yellow eggs, the chicken feet were added to the chicken curry. The giblets were spiced well, salted and fried in chicken fat or oil with sliced green chillies and onions, a pinch of turmeric, this was their comfort food.

The young men would sing jovially around the fire, singing traditional songs and playing the tabla.[4]. The drumbeats were their heartbeats. Thathas and Ayas, Nannas and Narnies all singing and enjoying the side dishes prepared.

Young girls adorned with beautiful brightly coloured bangles and anklets would join in the social gathering dancing to beat of the drums, dancing traditional dances. Women adorned themselves with earrings and bangles, ancient Indian folklore says that a tinkle of a bangle keeps negativity away. Anklets were worn by single girls, anklets have small bells that makes a pleasant sound, it is mostly to keep her safe from danger, if she sensed that she was in danger she would sound the alarm by tinkling the bells of her anklets until someone came to her rescue. Love was not enough; respect and trust were essential as was safety. These values of our ancestors still echo today from behind the scenes, from the realm of the spirit.

Gold is a precious metal greatly valued by our ancestors, in the Indian culture a woman wearing gold was considered auspicious. Gold is used in daily life and on special occasions, it holds a special significance in Indian culture. Gold jewellery is passed on from one generation to the next, from mothers to daughters.

Thathas and Ayas loved to chew betel nuts and betel leaves after a meal, it freshened their breath but stained their teeth and tongue red. However betel nut does not have health benefits. It is

---

[4] Tabla – a musical instrument

a tradition to serve betel nut and betel leaves at a wedding. The slices of betel nut is steamed and dried to make it less harmful. It is then cut into small pieces to which dried pieces of coloured coconut is added and tiny candy-coated fennel seeds as well, fennel seeds aid in digestion of food and prevents bloating.

Betel leaves has much health benefits. The oil from the betel leaf helps prevent tooth decay and keeps gums healthy. It prevents gums from bleeding and ensures overall dental health. Betel leaves helps relieve earache; betel leaf oil mixed with coconut is dropped into the sore ear for relief. Betel leaves act as an antiseptic, helps with arthritis, prevents and treats nosebleeds, supports wound healing. Squeeze juice of the leaves and apply it to the wound. It promotes blood clotting and healing.

After the Saturday night's celebration under the stars, our forefathers would say their goodnights and whisper a prayer of thanks. The wood fires had burnt out and this was the sign that it was time for bed. They were grateful they had each other, they would then head off to their shacks sleepily to lay their heads on the fluffy, down feathered pillows and mattresses made from pieces of cotton patches of old sarees sewn together to form a brightly coloured ethnic quilt called the 'Gudree'[5] with its mismatched mosaic patterns the gudree was comfort at its best, the inside of the gudree was stuffed with dried husks of mealies. They would get much needed rest and sleep which would rejuvenate them for the next day which was their day off however it was still a day of work as they would be tending to their vegetable gardens, but it was a labour of love.

---

[5] Gudree* quilt made from layers of old sarees or sheets

ANCESTRAL AROMAS - BASE FOR CURRIES

Shallots, onions, cumin/mustard seeds, green chillies, curry leaves, oil or ghee are all sautéed to flavour the oil.

AROMATIC SWEET SPICES

The aromatic sweet spices of cloves, cinnamon sticks, cardamom, nutmeg greatly enhanced the flavours of desserts such as rice puddings, semolina pudding and vermicelli, pancakes known as dosa and biscuits and cakes. No kitchen should be without these spices.

TIPS

BLENDED FRESH GREEN CHILLIES

1 cup chopped fresh green chillies

1 Tbsp salt

Process green chillies in a blender or food processor together with a tablespoon of oil. It makes for better preservation when stored in the refrigerator. This can be used when there's a scarcity of fresh chillies. Chillies add a sharpness to a vegetable or meat dish. It is an excellent marinate for meats that is going to be fried, braaied or grilled and together with ginger and garlic paste, a touch of masala and salt its aromas waft through the air making one look forward to mealtime.

9

AUTHENTIC ANCESTRAL INDIAN DISHES

THE BIRYANI DISH

Rice is a staple food of our ancestors, biryani was an authentic, exotic dish they would prepare for special occasions, today we still reserve biryani for special occasions such as weddings, birthdays or entertaining guests. Only the finest ingredients went into the vegetable biryani, fresh peas, green beans, gadra[6] beans, lentils, soft cooking potatoes that was roasted before adding to the biryani as this would prevent the potatoes from disintegrating, onions fried till it is golden brown.

SAFFRON - TALE OF THE FRAGRANT SPICE

Later when the merchant class or the rich upper-class Indians came to South Africa, they brought with them saffron. Saffron is an expensive, exotic pistil of a flower found in the snowy mountain ranges of India. Only the rich could afford to use this spice, it adds flavour and aroma thus enhancing the biryani dish adding an orange tint to white rice.

GINGER AND GARLIC

Besides adding flavour to a dish ginger and garlic tenderizes a meat dish and enhances the flavour of a fish dish. Ginger and

---

[6] Gadra beans - fresh beans from the bean pod

garlic freeze well. It is a wonderful tenderizer for tough cuts of meats, fish dishes taste better with garlic.

COCONUT CREAM OR COCONUT MILK

Coconut cream is excellent for making a thicker sauce or gravy, it adds flavour to a curry or biryani.

SPICES

Spices add a distinctive flavour to food and is pleasant to the senses of smell and taste. Garam masala is a blend of spices that is added to curries after the curry is cooked to enhance the flavour.

BUTTER GHEE

Clarified butter ghee keeps indefinitely making it ideal for our ancestors to store. Indian recipes highly recommend using ghee, it adds a distinct flavour to food prepared.

VEGETABLE BIRYANI

This is one of my favourite dishes. I add 400ml can of coconut cream instead of water.

INGREDIENTS

1 cup of rice

1 can of coconut cream 400 ml

125g lentils soaked in a cup of water for three hours

1 tsp salt, for your rice

1 tsp salt for your vegetables

125 ml oil

2 Tbsp Rombo Rossi masala or masala of your choice

3-star anise

4 cardamom pods bruised open a little

FOR EXTRA FLAVOUR

6 cloves

1 cinnamon stick

1 tsp cumin seeds

1 tsp mustard seeds

1 tsp fennel seeds

Half a teaspoon of saffron soaked in quarter cup of rose water (optional)

1 tomato thinly sliced

BROWN SPICES

1 tsp cumin powder

1 tsp fennel powder

1 tsp garam masala

1 tsp coriander powder

1 Tbsp ginger paste

1 Tbsp garlic paste

Half a cup of fresh cleaned, rinsed mint leaves

Half a cup of fresh, cleaned rinsed coriander leaves, chopped

1 sprig of curry leaves removed from the stalk and rinsed

VEGETABLES

2 carrots diced

1 cup diced green beans

1 250g punnet of mushrooms

1 cup frozen peas

2 green chillies sliced

2 medium potatoes and onions

METHOD

Peel and slice potatoes into 2 cm width rounds, fry in 125 ml oil until golden brown, remove the potatoes and keep aside.

Slice 2 medium size onions and fry in the oil that you fried your potatoes in, when it turns golden-brown in colour remove half of the fried onions and set aside.

To the remainder of the fried onions in the pot add in curry leaves, sliced green chillies, cumin, mustard and fennel seeds, star anise, cinnamon stick, cardamom, cloves and sauté this for a minute on medium heat. Add in ginger and garlic paste and cook for a minute, add in masala and stir well, add tomato and cook for a minute.

Add in frozen peas, vegetables that you have rinsed and drained, there is no need for you to rinse the peas, add in rice that is rinsed and drained, add in rinsed and drained lentils, add salt and coconut cream and stir well. Cook for half an hour after which you add the fried potatoes, the other fried onion that you set aside, saffron and rose water, mint/coriander leaves and brown spices and mix well. If you find that the biryani is sticking to the bottom the pot add in a little water until your lentils and rice is tender. Serve with yoghurt salad or carrot salad.

CARROT SALAD

2 carrots cleaned, rinsed and grated

1 small onion thinly sliced

1 green chilli finely chopped

Juice of 1 lemon

1 sprig coriander rinsed and finely chopped

quarter tsp salt, mix well

CHICKEN BIRYANI

Chicken Biryani

Made in the potjie pot (cast iron pot) over open wood fire. The wood fire is the most important element for this recipe.

Wood fire cooking is more than a method of cooking, it's the smells from the wood fire that goes into the cooking that takes it to another level of gastronomic taste bud pleasure. Use natural wood, chopped into pieces. Different types of wood give off different smells, example wood from fruit trees such cherry trees give off a fruity smell. Use a firelighter to start the fire and place pieces of wood and let it burn down until the coals are a grey tone. This usually takes about 20 minutes, spread coals around with a pair of tongs. Place pot on the hot coals and add oil, brown chicken portions and remove from pot, set aside in a large mixing bowl. At this stage remove pot from the heat as you do not want to overheat the oil.

INGREDIENTS

1kg chicken portions browned slightly but not fully cooked

1 sprig curry leaves

6 Tbsp oil

2 Tbsp ginger and garlic paste

2 green chillies sliced in half

3 onions sliced

125 ml plain yogurt

1 cup of rice soaked for thirty minutes

2 tsp salt

Fresh coriander to garnish

1 fried onion for garnishing

BROWN SPICES

1 tsp cumin powder

1 tsp coriander powder

1 tsp fennel powder

1 tsp garam masala

2 Tbsp curry masala of your choice

WHOLE SPICES

3-star anise

2 cinnamon sticks

6 cardamom pods

1 tsp fennel seeds

6 cloves

3 bay leaves

1 tsp cumin seeds

Khada masala

METHOD

Marinate chicken portions with all the spices and 1 tsp salt and yogurt. Place potjie pot back of the coals and fry onions, green chillies, curry leaves in fry onion until it is golden in colour, add in the ginger and garlic paste and fry for one minute on low heat, add in marinated chicken and cover and cook for 20 minutes. Rinse and cook rice in 2 cups of water together with 1 cinnamon stick and 1 tsp salt until almost done and there's no water in the rice. Add in cooked rice on top of the cooking chicken and let it cook for about 10 minutes. Remove from heat and garnish with fresh coriander and fried onions. Serve with yogurt salad.

YOGURT SALAD

500ml plain yoghurt

1 cup mint leaves cleaned and rinsed

1 green chilli chopped

1 clove garlic

Small piece of onion finely chopped

Quarter tsp salt

Half a cup cucumber cut into small pieces

METHOD

Blend half the yoghurt, mint leaves, chilli, and garlic until it is smooth, remove from the blender into your serving bowl, add in onion, cucumber and salt and mix well and serve with biryani.

CORNISH CHICKEN BIRYANI

Aunty Pam Varthen's famous Cornish chicken biryani which she prepared for special occasions such as Mother's Day or Christmas day to take to our favourite picnic spot, the Japanese Gardens in Durban.

INGREDIENTS

1 kg Cornish chicken pieces

Quarter cup lentils pre-soaked for 3 hours

1 cup rice pre-soaked for one hour

2 Tbsp ginger and garlic paste

1 sprig curry leaves, leaves removed and rinsed

2 green chillies sliced in half

Half a cup of green peas

1 tomato chopped

Half a cup of fresh chopped coriander leaves

Half a cup of fresh mint leaves

2 sprigs of thyme

3 Tbsp butter

3 Tbsp oil

2 medium size potatoes

2 onions sliced finely

METHOD

Heat butter/oil in a medium size pot until fairly hot and fry 2 potatoes that is peeled and quartered and lightly salted, fry until golden brown, (you can fry potatoes in a nonstick pan or air fryer for your convenience) remove from butter/oil and set aside in the same oil fry 2 onions that has been finely sliced with curry leaves and 2 green chillies that has been sliced in half, fry until the onion is golden brown.

MARINATE FOUR CHICKEN PORTIONS

Rinse and drain chicken portions, add in the 2 fried onions, 2 tsp salt ginger and garlic paste, whole spices of 1 cinnamon stick, 2 bay leaf, 2-star anise, 3 cardamom pods, 6 cloves, 1 Tbsp fennel seeds, 1 tsp cumin seeds, then add in the brown spice powders of 1 tsp biryani masala (optional) 1 tsp fennel powder, 1 tsp cumin powder, 1 tsp coriander powder, 1 tsp garam masala, chopped tomato. Mix all this well and leave to marinate for an hour.

After one hour add in the marinated chicken to the pot that has the butter/oil in which you fried your potatoes and onions. Cover and simmer for 45 minutes before adding rice and lentils. Rinse rice and lentils, drain, add in a tsp of salt and add to the simmering chicken, add peas, fresh herbs of coriander, mint and thyme and half a cup of water and mix well until all the water has evaporated. Garnish with fresh coriander leaves. Serve with a carrot salad or yogurt salad.

CASHEW NUT PESTO

250g cashew nuts

1 cup mint leaves cleaned, rinsed and drained

Half a tsp of tamarind concentrates mixed with 3 Tbsp of water

Half a teaspoon of salt

3 Tbsp olive oil or oil of your choice

Blend cashew nuts, mint, salt and tamarind water to form a paste, if it is too thick add in a Tbsp of water a time until you get a desired consistency. Once well blended remove from blender into a serving bowl and add in olive oil and mix well, serve on toasted bread of your choice, crackers or have a tablespoon or two with your meals.

TIP

CASTOR OIL SEED STORY

There was a story that was often mentioned at a social get together and that was the 'castor oil story' a group of teenage cousins found a field of ripe castor oil seeds, they tasted the seeds and it was delicious, unfortunately they did not know of the side effects of the castor oil seeds. They all became extremely ill with a runny tummy that did not stop running and had to be rushed to hospital to the emergency room in a tractor.

10

ANCESTRALS FOODS - OFFALS

Offal such as sheep head, trotters, liver, tripe were foods often eaten our forefathers. These foods were cheap and affordable. They would buy fish heads which was the cheapest part of the fish and make a tasty fish curry served with thick mealie meal porridge known as sangiti* or kali in vernacular or pap in Afrikaans. Sheep trotters cooked with dried beans made a healthy bone broth. Tripe which resembles a towel was a delicacy they greatly enjoyed by our ancestors.

Sangiti* thick mealie meal porridge

TRIPE AND DHAL
RECIPE BY AUNT ROSLYN JAMES
INGREDIENTS

500g tripe

2 tsp salt

1 cup pea dhal, (dried split peas)

Half a tsp asafoetida

125 ml oil

1 onion sliced finely

2 tomatoes grated

1 sprig curry leaf rinsed and leaves removed

2 green chillies sliced in half

2 tsp garlic paste

2 tsp ginger paste

3 Tbsp masala

Fresh coriander to garnish

Brown spices

1 tsp garam masala

1 tsp fennel powder

1 tsp cumin powder

1 tsp coriander powder

WHOLE SPICES

2-star anise

1 cinnamon stick

METHOD

Cook tripe with 1 tsp of salt for about 3 hours until soft and tender, keep aside. Use a pressure cooker if you have one.

Cook dried split peas (pea dhal) with 1 tsp of salt and half a tsp asafoetida until it's tender and keep aside.

In a medium pot, on medium heat add oil, when oil is sufficiently hot add in sliced onions and fry until it's translucent, then add in curry leaves, sliced green chillies, ginger and garlic paste and stir for a few seconds thereafter add in spices and stir, add in tomatoes and cook for one minute. And in the cooked tripe and dhal and cook for a further 15 minutes, add little water to the consistency of the gravy you prefer. Garnish with coriander and serve with rice.

11

ANCESTRAL MEDICINAL SPICES

RASUM DHAL - SPLIT PEA DHAL 'KING SOUP'

Staple Mixed Herbs and Spices

A favourite with potato curry and rice this soup is an immunity booster and an authentic, traditional soup. Rasum has many health benefits. It clears the respiratory tracts and helps relieve colds and flus making you feel a lot better.

INGREDIENTS - PEA SOUP

2 cups water

1 cup dried split peas (pea dhal) rinsed

1 tsp salt

Half a tsp asafoetida

Half a tsp of turmeric powder

Cook pea dhal in a pressure cooker or stove until its soft, set aside

INGREDIENTS - RASUM OR KING SOUP

2 Tbsp oil

1 onion finely sliced

1 tomato grated

1 sprig curry leaves rinsed, and leaves separated

2 sprigs coriander rinsed and chopped

1 tsp salt

half a teaspoon turmeric powder

4 dried chillies broken into pieces

In the pestle and mortar pound,

1 tsp peppercorns,

1 tsp cumin seeds,

1 tsp mustard seeds,

4 cloves garlic,

Spices does not have to be finely ground and garlic can be lightly smashed.

METHOD

Fry onion until it's translucent add in garlic, curry leaves, dried chillies, and turmeric and fry further until onions turn golden brown, add in tomato and cook for three minutes, add ground spices of peppercorn/cumin/mustard and cook for one minute after which you add in the mushy cooked dhal, add in a little water it all depends on how thick you like the dhal to be, it's better to add in a little at a time. Garnish with fresh coriander. Recipe for potato curry can be found 'Comfort Foods' Yvonne Singh's South Indian dosa recipe with potato curry, page 102.

TIP

HONEY

Honey is known a 'liquid gold' in food terminology, potent medicinal liquid gold for the healing of mankind. Honey keeps indefinitely and does not lose its nutritional value. Honey is easily assimilated into the bloodstream and generates energy quickly without shocking the system. Honey has a high mineral content is a powerful germicide killing of any bacteria that settles on it. Honey comes in a variety of flavours depending on the seasonal flowers of the environment, whether it's the subtle fragrance of citrus blossoms or the sweet perfume of rose blossoms may the golden liquid be found in your kitchen cupboard together with all your other essential items.

"I did not know this. I have local honey in my tea, always using a metal spoon. Did you know that honey contains live enzymes? Did you know that in contact with a metal spoon these enzymes die? The best way to eat honey is with a wooden spoon; if you don't have a wooden spoon, use a plastic spoon. Did you know that honey contains a substance that helps the brain think better? Did you know that honey is one of the few foods on earth that alone can sustain human life? Did you know that bees saved people from starvation in Africa? A spoonful of honey is enough to keep a man alive for twenty-four hours? Did you know that propolis produced by bees is one of the most powerful natural antibiotics? Did you know that honey has no expiry date? Did you that a bee lives less than forty days, visits at least a thousand flowers and produces less than a teaspoon of honey, a lifetime of for the honey bee? Thank you, precious bee!

(Source: Robin Jackson) Much respect and gratitude goes out to the humble honey bee for the precious honey that we consume.

12

ANCESTRAL REMEDIES

TRADITIONAL SPA TREATMENT

EUCALYPTUS LEAF BATH - NATURAL HERBAL FACIAL STEAM TO UNBLOCK A CONJESTED NASAL PASSAGE

Leaves from the eucalyptus tree is boiled in a large pot, a towel is held over the person who has the cold, as soon as the person complains the towel is removed, rubbed with vapour rub and put into bed. This treatment decongests a blocked nose helps heal a head cold. The eucalyptus leaf bath is also used to bath woman who had just given birth. The aromatic herbs are soothing and comforting.

HOT GINGER TEA

2cm piece of ginger root

1 tsp honey

3 Tbsp lemon juice

If you have a scratchy sore throat a hot cup of ginger tea with a teaspoon of honey and a squeeze of lemon juice helps. Ginger tea helps eradicate mucous built up. Clean, rinse and grate a piece of ginger about two centimetres in length and two centimetres in width, place into a mug to which boiled water is added, sip this and enjoy as a tea.

ANCESTRAL MEDICINAL SPICE - BIRTH MASALA

What is birth masala? Birth masala is a combination of medicinal potent herbs and spices with anti-inflammatory and anti-bacterial properties. It is brown in colour and greatly enhances the flavour of fresh chicken curry. Our ancestors have used these blend of ancient spices for centuries especially for woman who had just given birth hence the name 'birth masala.' Birth masala has many benefits, it heals the body, building strength and immunity. It helps in breastfeeding making healthy milk for the baby, lactating mom's produce more milk when given a delicious chicken curry made with birth masala.

The main ingredients in birth masala are cumin seeds, coriander seeds, dried ginger, cinnamon sticks, carom, fennel, fenugreek seeds and turmeric. These spices are roasted and ground into a fine powder and stored in airtight containers and kept in a cool, dark cupboard. In South Africa a bowl of comforting chicken soup made with birth masala helps one recover more quickly from a cold or flu, it is because of the turmeric and ginger added to it. It also increases metabolism and aids in digestion.

I consider this spice an essential in every kitchen cupboard. My grandmother made this spice for me when I had my first child, she used a metal pestle and mortar to pound the spices and then sifted the spices through a muslin cloth, a week later after the birth of my daughter she passed away, I appreciate her kindness of making this special spice for me even though she was very ill. My love and gratitude go to my beloved grandmother.

INGREDIENTS - BIRTH MASALA CURRY

Homemade birth masala

1 small onion sliced

1 small tomato grated

2 green chillies sliced in half

a sprig of curry leaf, leaves removed and rinsed

A few cloves of garlic lightly crushed

BROWN SPICES

1 tsp of cumin powder

1 tsp of coriander powder

1 tsp garam masala which is a blend of spices

1 tsp of fennel powder

2 Tbsp of birth masala spice

1 Tbsp of curry powder (masala)

2 Tbsp of ginger and garlic paste

1 kg chicken cleaned and cut into portions

4 Tbsp oil

1 Tbsp salt

METHOD

To a pot add in the oil on medium heat, add sliced onion and fry this until it's translucent, add in ginger/garlic paste, green chillies, curry leaves and stir. Add in brown spices and masala, mix well and simmer for thirty seconds. Add in chicken pieces, salt and stir well. Add in grated tomato and cook for a further five minutes. Thereafter add in half a cup of water and cook for twenty minutes, garnish with fresh coriander leaves and serve with rice.

INSIGHTS

As the years passed our forefathers became frustrated with the way in which they were treated, it became too much for them to bear, so they complained of their living conditions and abuse. News of the atrocities went back to the authorities in India known as the 'Coolie Commission.' The indentured labourer was physically, mentally, financially exhausted. Every day was a struggle. Eventually their employers were forced to make living conditions better for them. Ablution blocks were built with eastern flush toilets. Water was supplied from boreholes. Water had to be boiled and carried in buckets to the public bathroom for bathing.

One ablution block consisted of two toilets and two bathrooms for men and two toilets and two bathrooms for women. One ablution block of every twenty houses. It was only in the seventies that a coal stove geyser was installed that heated up the water in no time and made life easier and the burden lighter. Households took turns to start up the fire that heated the water every day, someone had to keep an eye on the fire to keep it from going out. They would gather pines cones which was in abundance or chop wood which was provided for them. Sometimes they would gather sugarcane stalks that had been run over by tractors on the road. These would burn very well and quickly heated up the water.

The landowners planted ginger on the land. Plantations of ginger graced the landscapes, there were fields of turmeric as well. Ginger and turmeric were brought from India and so was banana plants. Stories were told by my grandparents of a huge python living in the banana plantation, someone had seen the snake slither into the plantation. Fortunately for the constrictor it was taken to a snake sanctuary by snake handlers much to the relief of those living in the area.

Our forefathers were categorized as African Indians, they now received a food ration of dried split peas, dried beans, sunflower oil, rice, mealie meal, flour and sugar and life became easier. Meals were provided on special days to the community for whosoever wished to partake. It was usually during the harvest festival being celebrated where they gave thanks for the bountiful harvest. Those who celebrated contributed a portion of the harvest and this was cooked and shared, even with those that did not have anything to give. It was mostly pumpkin, cabbage, loofahs that was prepared and served with rice, fermented mealie meal porridge or roti.

There was now a community hall for functions and weddings, tasty biryanis were served at these functions followed by semolina pudding a delightful dessert which was tastier when eaten from the same plate as the delicious biryani. The hosts would always prepare extra for those less fortunate who would stand outside and wait until all the guests had eaten and then go inside the dining area to eat.

Our forefathers lived with integrity and immense respect for each other. The community church would host an annual event a week before Christmas for the Sunday school children. Meals were provided for the children and they would receive a Christmas gift lighting up their faces like a Christmas tree, the children looked forward to these special days eagerly. On food ration day each household would receive currant buns and fruit cake loaves for Christmas.

There was a local clinic providing services for the sick. On a Thursday they would give out pronutro cereal to children, the children would have to take along their bowls or packets to collect the cereal. These were the humble beginnings of our forefathers, strong and resilient. It is because of their strong work ethics, discipline and not giving up that we are here today. We honour their legacy and steadfastness. The merchant class were able to buy farms and plant sugarcane. They would go on to build schools for the surrounding districts.

Children would walk to school. Universities and colleges were built for children to further educate themselves. Some outstanding students would receive bursaries. Many students did extremely well and appeared in the top ten list of the brightest students in the country, they studied further to become doctors, teachers and lawyers.

EDUCATIONAL LEGACY

There are many institutions that bear the name ML Sultan, today we celebrate the remarkable contribution M L Sultan had on education in KwaZulu Natal. He founded the M L Sultan Technikon in 1941 in Durban. His vision was 'Education Is the Key To Freedom.' M L Sultan was a leading tertiary provider. M L Sultan arrived in South Africa in 1890, despite humble beginnings he became a successful businessman. His dedication to education was remarkable. His legacy lives on through multitudes of students who benefit from high quality education.

Let us not forget the nannies, janitors and domestic workers who sent their children to school no matter how poor they were. The cooks who worked for the rich landowners would bring home leftover meals that was prepared for their landowners. The cooks would prepare delicious bread and butter pudding from the bread no longer used at their employer's house

THE USE OF NANNIES

The use of nannies and domestic workers was popular in those days, maintaining boundaries of class, race and gender

Women were used as household servants. They were used for spinning, weaving and dressmaking. Indentured servants played an important part in the development of the economy.

STORY OF TEATIME

As South African Indians we pride ourselves with beautiful tea sets to have our daily rituals of tea including tea trays with beautifully embroidered tea tray cloths. No Indian home is without beautiful tea set. Having your afternoon tea while doing their embroidery was a favourite past time of our grandmothers.

Tea is a delicious golden beverage enjoyed by our ancestors. It was a staple beverage of our ancestors. The favourite tea consumed by our ancestors was masala tea which consists of a blend of aromatic spices such as dried ginger, cinnamon, cloves, and cardamom are used to make masala tea. A delicious cup of masala tea with mealies and potatoes that has been cooked in the embers of the burnt-out wood fire was a treat.

EMBROIDERY

I learnt to embroider when I was in grade four, it was a lesson in life skills. Girls were taught to sew, knit and embroider. I have never lost my passion for embroidery, sewing, crocheting and knitting, I have improved a lot over the years. I embroidered a tea tray cloth with strawberries inspired by the strawberry farm I grew up in, in the seventies in the Kwa Zulu Natal midlands.

I learnt to sew, crochet and embroider from my mom and granny as well. Our grandmothers cultivated life skills of sewing, knitting, crocheting, embroidery and reading. They would pass by a clothing boutique and see the beautiful outfits on display, they would go home and replicate the pattern. They were skilful that way. In the sixties and seventies movies were shown to the communities using a projector, the movie was projected onto a white wall, you had to carry along your own chairs and benches to sit on and a warm crocheted blanket to cover your shoulders as you enjoyed the movie night in the open air.

Our grandmothers would make us ponchos just by watching movies, they could create the exact same design of the poncho as seen in the movie. They enjoyed watching a variety of movies from country and western to musicals and movies from the Indian cinema. They also participated in a wide variety of sport such as soccer and cricket, my dad played cricket at school. Every district had a soccer field. A saree queen contest was held annually, a winner was chosen by how elegantly she modelled the saree and how beautiful the saree looked.

LANTERNS

These lamps were used by our forefathers to light up their homes so that fumble in the dark.

13

ANCESTRAL SWEET MEATS

CHEVDA, MITHAI, CHILLI BITES AND SWEETMEATS – SNACKS

Sweet Meat

Sweetmeats consist of a variety of snacks such as jelebi,* ludoo,* gulab jamuns* and coconut ice. Chilli bites called bajias* and chevda* is a mix of toasted slices of coloured coconut, mithai* and roasted or fried peanuts. There's also murku* a crunchy spiral shaped snack made from maize flour. All these tasty traditional Indian snacks are part of the Indian culture. Our forefathers would carry a packet of mithai when visiting families. These tasty treats are made for functions, weddings and festivals together with gulgulas* (fritters)

Spicy dhal fritters called vedas*, children would look forward to their grandparents bringing them these snacks.

Jelebi* - sweet syrup filled spiral sweet meat

Ludoo* - sweet round dessert

Gulab jamuns* - elongated fritter dipped in a syrup that has rose water in it, the word gulab* - means rose.

Bajias* - chilli bites

Mithai* - sweetmeats

Murku* - a crunchy spiral shaped savoury snack made from mealie meal and spices such cumin seeds.

Gulgulas* - sweet fritters

GULAB JAMUNS - INDIAN DOUGHNUT
RECIPE BY CHANDINI VARTHEN

This recipe was given to me by Chandini Varthen who makes the most delicious baked treats, who is quick and efficient in the kitchen.

INGREDIENTS

1 cup all-purpose flour plus a quarter cup for dusting

1 Tbsp semolina

1 Tbsp butter ghee or butter

1 tsp baking powder

Half a tsp bicarb of soda

Half a tsp of cardamom powder

170ml condensed milk

300ml oil for frying

METHOD

Mix all ingredients until a soft dough is formed. Pinch out small pieces of dough and roll into a ball in the palms of your hands, then roll the ball into an elongated shape about 4 or 5cm long. Heat oil in a medium size pan on medium to high heat. When oil is fairly hot drop in a small piece of dough into the oil to see if it's ready for frying, if the oil is bubbling the gulab jamuns are ready to fry. At this stage you can lower heat a bit to medium. Fry gulab jamuns until golden brown in colour. Remove from oil and place on paper towels for the excess oil to be absorbed.

SYRUP FOR GULAB JAMUNS

2 cups sugar

2 cups water

1 Tbsp lemon juice

Boil sugar, water and lemon juice until syrup is sticky between two fingers. Dip gulab jamuns in syrup and roll in desiccated coconut. Enjoy with a cup of masala tea.

14

SAVOURY DELIGHTS

SAMOSA - triangular shaped savoury or sweet snack

Savoury Delights

Samosa is an Indian snack which originated in India. Samosas are found in almost every Indian take-away and restaurant in South Africa. Samosas are a perfect travel snack and is ideal for a lunch box, a party platter or just as a tea time treat. Easy to eat and economical, many fillings can go into a samosa from vegetarian fillings of cooked, mashed potato with fresh herbs of mint and coriander, hint of green chilli to sweetcorn and cheese, this savoury snack appeals to the taste buds making it hard to just enjoy one.

There's a variety of meat filled samosas to choose such as chicken mince, mutton or beef mince. Fresh mint, coriander, onion, ginger/garlic paste, spices and green chilli enhances the flavour of the fillings and is an essential to the filling. Samosas are served with a dipping sauce such as Mrs Balls chutney. Soya mince is another favourite filling substituting meat mince as a filling for samosas.

The chocolate filled samosa makes a tasty dessert treat, when fried the chocolate quickly melts inside and upon the first bite causes an avalanche of chocolaty flavour in your mouth.

BAKED CHILLI BITES
BY SARAVATHY CHELLAN
INGREDIENTS

1 cup gram flour

2 tsp baking powder

2 tsp salt

1 tsp cumin powder

1 tsp asafoetida (hing)

1 chopped onion

3-4 green chillies finely chopped

A few spring onion finely chopped

A few sprigs fresh coriander leaves chopped

1 egg beaten

100ml olive oil

Water to make a thick batter

METHOD

Spray muffin tray with 'spray and cook' or grease lightly with melted butter or oil. Fill chilli bite batter halfway as in each muffin tray pocket as filling to top can cause mixture to overflow whilst baking. Bake at 200 degree for 20 minutes.

INGREDIENTS - CHILLI BITES (BHAJIAS)

1 cup gram flour

1 Tbsp cake flour

1 medium onion finely chopped

1 small potato grated

1 tsp cumin powder

1 tsp coriander powder

3 green chillies finely chopped

1 tsp salt

1 tsp baking powder (optional)

1 bunch fresh coriander leaves chopped

Quarter cup finely chopped shallots

1 litre sunflower cooking oil

METHOD

In a large mixing bowl add all ingredients and add in little water at a time until you a thick batter. Heat oil in a small to medium sized pot, medium to high heat. Test the oil by dropping in a small quantity of batter in, if the batter is bubbling in the oil the chilli bites are ready to fry. Drop in dessertspoonsful of chilli bite batter into oil.

Spread evenly around the pot but touching. Take care not to overcrowd the pot leaving enough space in between chilli bites to allow for turning. Turn over chilli bites once they turn golden brown in colour and when the other side is the same golden-brown colour. Remove from oil and place on paper towels, serve while hot with a dipping sauce such as Mrs Balls chutney.

TIP - VARIATIONS OF CHILLI BITES

Add a cup of chopped lettuce or watercress or baby spinach. Thinly sliced aubergine dipped in this batter and fried is delicious. Thinly sliced potato dipped in batter and fried till golden brown, in this case omit the grated potato from the recipe. Cut unripe jackfruit into wedges, dip in batter and fry until golden brown. Okra cut in half, dipped in batter and fried until golden brown.

INGREDIENTS - SOUTH AFRICAN VEDA OR SPLIT PEA FRITTERS

2 cups dried split peas

4 green chillies

1 tsp cumin seeds

1 tsp fennel seeds

2 cloves garlic

2 cm piece ginger root

1 onion finely chopped

2 tsp salt

1 cup fresh coriander leaves finely chopped

Half a tsp turmeric powder

1 tsp baking powder

1 Tbsp red chilli flakes

METHOD

2 cups dried split peas covered and soaked overnight. The next day rinse and drain the split peas well. Place in a food processor together with 4 green chillies, 1 tsp cumin seeds, 1 tsp fennel seeds, 2 cloves garlic, a 2 cm piece of ginger and blend well, add in a few tablespoons of water at a time to make the blending process more efficient. Blend into a smooth paste. The mixture must not be watery but firm enough to form a round shape in the palm of your hand. It should be of a paste consistency.

Remove from blender into a mixing bowl and add in 1 cup of fresh chopped coriander, 1 onion finely chopped, 2 tsp salt, half a teaspoon of turmeric powder, 1 tsp baking powder, 1 Tbsp red chilli flakes and mix well.

Heat enough oil in a medium pot for deep frying. When oil is sufficiently hot place a small piece of veda* mix into the oil to test if it's ready, if the oil is bubbling that means your vedas* are ready to be fried. Take a small amount of veda* mix, the size of a golf ball and place it on the palm of your hand and slightly flatten it using your other hand. Pierce a hole in the centre using your finger. Carefully place into hot oil, continue placing more into the hot oil but avoid overcrowding. Fry until golden brown and crisp. Remove from oil and place on paper towels for excess oil to be absorbed. Enjoy while it's still hot with a refreshing cold drink or a hot cup of masala tea.

TIP

Vedas and samosas can be baked in the oven or fried in the air fryer as a healthier option.

15

GULGULA FILLED WITH DHAL AND FRESH COCONUT

SOMETHING SWEET - BY KELLY MARKEY

One of my favourite memories is growing up in Tugela Pardianargar Township. My neighbour was Telegu and they made the most delicious stuff for their prayer offerings. My all-time best loved treasure was gulgula[7] filled with dhal and sliced fresh coconut. I do love anything with coconut perhaps I am biased but do this and let your taste buds do the voting. This recipe is from memory muscle and courtesy of my fine neighbours Aunty Freda and her daughters Brenda and June whom have all passed on but their legacy lives on!

INGREDIENTS

1 cup urad dhal

1 cup thinly sliced coconut

1 cup jaggery (or sugar)

1 cup all-purpose flour

quarter tsp baking powder

half tsp cardamom powder, oil for frying

---

[7] gulgula - sweet fritters

METHOD

Soak dhal in water for 4 to 5 hours, then drain the water. Grind dhal into a smooth paste. In a mixing bowl combine the ground dhal paste, sliced fresh coconut and jaggery. Mix well and roll into small round balls. Add all-purpose flour, baking powder, cardamom powder and mix well to form a thick batter. Heat oil in a deep-frying pan over medium heat. Test oil with a small drop of batter, if the oil bubbles your gulgulas are ready for frying. Take the dhal balls and drop into the batter, ensure the batter fully covers the dhal. Carefully drop the gulgula into hot oil and fry until golden brown and crispy. Remove the fried gulgulas from the oil and place on paper towels to absorb excess oil. Serve hot.

KOEKSUSTERS - THE 'TWISTED SISTER' OF THE DOUGHNUT

Koeksusters.[8] is a traditional South African tea time treat made of fried dough, thereafter dipped in cold syrup and sprinkled with desiccated coconut. My neighbour in Secunda, Mpumalanga Elsa Byleveld always made a batch for my son Ian, who loved koeksusters. Crispy on the outside and soft, chewy and syrupy on the inside, delicious. We called the koeksusters 'Tannie.[9] Elsa's koeksusters'. Tannie Elsa also made the most divine moist chocolate cake, her secret was, a cup of strong black coffee added to the mixture.

I'm going to share with you my favourite koeksuster recipe, the Cape Malay Koeksuster. I got the recipe from my dearest friend Priscilla Lottering who was born in Cape Town but now lives in the Mpumalanga Province.

---

[8] Koeksuster syrupy doughnut
[9] Tannie - aunty

Recipes of My Heritage

CAPE MALAY KOEKSUSTER
RECIPE BY PRISCILLA LOTTERING
INGREDIENTS

4 cups flour

Half a teaspoon salt

1 tsp cardamom powder

1 tsp ginger powder

1 tsp cinnamon powder

1 tsp baking soda

Quarter cup sugar

1 packet dry yeast (10g)

100g butter

2 eggs

Quarter cup oil

Half cup milk

1 large potato boiled and mashed

METHOD

Mix flour, baking soda, spices, yeast and sugar well. Mash potato well, add oil and butter to mash potato and mix well. Add in eggs one at a time alternating with milk. Finally add in flour to make a soft dough. Place dough on a lightly floured surface and knead until it's smooth and pliable. Place dough in a lightly greased bowl and cover with dish cloth and set aside for one hour. In the meantime, prepare the syrup.

SYRUP

3 cups of flour

2 cups of water

1 stick cinnamon

Bring this to boil until all the sugar has dissolved thoroughly. Make this syrup ahead of time and leave in the refrigerator to chill.

Lightly flour surface, place dough on floured surface. Take out a small quantity of dough about the size of a golf ball and shape into an oval shape, place on floured surface to rise, make sure to leave a space between each koeksuster* to allow it to rise. Once the koeksuster* is rested and well risen it is ready to fry.

Heat two litres of sunflower oil in a deep pot on medium to high heat, test the oil by placing a small piece of dough into the oil, if the small piece of dough is bubbling in the oil the koeksusters* are ready to fry. Place the koeksusters* in the hot oil and fry until brown in colour. You will know when your koeksusters* are ready when there are less bubbles and they are bouncy and buoyant. Remove from the oil and place on paper towels to absorb excess oil. By now the kitchen should be filled with all the aromas of the spices used in the koeksusters*. Dip koeksusters* in syrup and sprinkle with desiccated coconut and enjoy.

Koeksuster* - syrupy doughnut

BAKER'S CHOICE ASSORTED BISCUITS

Baker's choice assorted biscuits are an all-time traditional favourite in all households. The two kg boxes are sold especially during the Christmas season and everyone had their favourite. Mom would like the wafer, dad would prefer the ginger nuts, granny loved the eet-sum-mor shortbread that she would dunk into her tea, the kids loved them all. There was also a stash or Baker's Marie biscuits and cream crackers in mom's pantry, Marie biscuits with a layer of butter or cream crackers with butter and a slice of cheese was a tea time treat. When our uncles and aunts visited us, they would always bring us a box of Baker's choice assorted biscuits and a packet of Beacon 'nut puffs' sweets, we the children enjoyed their visits, sometimes our visiting relatives gave us a twenty-cent coin before leaving. With the twenty-cent coin you could buy a packet of fresh potato chips, a packet of chewing gums and sweets.

16

LEKKER BRAAI

FRIDAY NIGHT GATHERING AROUND THE RADIO

The Dutch term, "Braaivleis," meaning "grilled meat," became integrated into South African culture.

When I was growing up there was no television, I remember the first time I saw a television set was in 1975 through the window of a furniture store. I was in awe, we never owned a television of our own, maybe it was not affordable. In the meantime, we had the radio that entertained us. The 'Mind of Tracy Dark' a psychic who could predict and solve crime, and 'Squad Cars' a South African Police

Department fighting crime, sponsored by General Motors every Friday night at seven thirty. The show would always start with a police siren, screeching of brakes and shooting, most likely at a suspect at the scene of a crime. The narrator would start by saying, "Names have been changed to protect innocent people involved." The music became dramatic as the suspect was being caught leaving us listeners on the edge of our seats.

A nostalgic trip down memory lane listening to the 'Mind of Tracy Dark' a Psychic detective on Springbok Radio. Before the show started there would always be an advert for the sponsor 'Chevrolet,'

"South Africa what's your favourite meal?"

"Braaivleis!"

"Sport?"

"Rugby!"

"Weather?"

"Sunny Skies!"

"Car?"

"Chevrolet!"

"Now sing it South Africa, we love braaivleis, rugby, sunny skies and Chevrolet."

The lightning and thunderstorms were paid actors for this epic drama. We would sit wide eyed, engrossed and let our imaginations run and jump suddenly to the slightest noise outside. There was no surround sound just the lightning and thunder on a stormy night. The whole family would gather near the radio listening attentively to Tracy Dark solving crimes with her psychic powers. These are treasured moments spent as a family. I cherish these memories in the closet my heart, memories of 'family closeness.'

TIP
BRAAI SIDE DISHES

Large brown mushrooms – season with a sprinkle of salt, a dollop of butter, a sprinkle of grated cheese – place on braai stand, however not on high heat.

Cheese, tomato, onion and a light spread of monkey gland sauce – grill on the braai stand, low heat.

Wash whole potatoes, cover skin with butter and bake in a moderate 180-degree oven until soft and tender, cut open and sprinkle seasoning, salt, butter or sour cream.

CHOKA ROASTED EGGPLANT
RECIPE BY KELLY MARKEY

This is an excellent side dish for a braai or filling for a party platter with an assortment of breads such as sliced and toasted ciabatta or wraps.

My dad made the most sumptuous choka[10]. The art of choka making traces back through generations, woven into the cultural tapestry of Indian traditions. Passed down from Ancestors who harmonized with the land, chocka preparation is steeped in reverence for nature and culinary ingenuity. From selecting the finest ingredients to mastering the delicate balance of heat and time, each step in the process honours wisdom of those who came before. Through fire-side gatherings and familial teachings, the legacy of choka making persists, bridging the past with the present in a celebration of heritage and flavour.

Indulge in the savoury delight of my dad's delicious aubergine choka, lovingly roasted in crackling flames. Each bite transports

---

[10] Choka - Roasted Aubergine

you to a world of rich flavours and ancestral traditions, a culinary journey infused with warmth and heritage. Experience the essence of cultural mastery in every mouthful. I love the fresh flavours infused with the smoke, this recipe lives on from dad: Rampershad Ramlucken from Tugela, South Africa.

INGREDIENTS

2 large aubergines (eggplant)

2 tomatoes diced

2 cloves garlic minced

2 Tbsp olive oil

Salt and pepper to taste

Fresh herbs such as parsley or cilantro.[11] for garnish

2-4 green chillies depending on how hot you would prefer it

Juice of 1 lemon

METHOD

Prepare fire and let it burn down to hot coals. Pierce the aubergines all over with a fork to prevent them from bursting while roasting. Place the whole aubergines directly onto hot coals of the fire, rotating them occasionally to ensure even cooking. Roast for about 15 to 20 minutes or until skins are charred and the flesh is soft. While the aubergines are roasting, mix olive oil and lemon juice in a salad bowl, add the diced onion and garlic, mix well. Once the aubergines are roasted carefully remove them from the fire using tongs and allow them to cool slightly. Peel of the charred skin from aubergines and discard. Chop the roasted flesh into small pieces and mash with a fork and transfer to the salad bowl. Stir in the diced tomatoes and

---

[11] Cilantro - Fresh Coriander

season with salt and pepper to taste, garnish with fresh herbs and serve hot as a delicious side dish or as a main course with crusty bread or rice. Enjoy!

MONKEY GLAND SAUCE

When I first heard of monkey gland sauce, I thought that it was a sauce made from 'monkey's glands and I refused to eat it until and friend convinced me that it was not made from monkey's gland and gave me the recipe to prove it.

INGREDIENTS

3 Tbsp Worcester sauce

1 minced onion

1 Tbsp tomato sauce

1 tsp mustard

3 Tbsp vinegar

3 Tbsp Mrs Balls Chutney

Combine all ingredients together and mix well. Use as a marinate for meat and chicken when braaing.

INGREDIENTS - CHICKEN ON SKEWERS

1 kg chicken breasts or deboned thighs cut into 2 cm by 2cm cubes

2 Tbsp ginger and garlic paste

3 Tbsp yogurt

2 Tbsp olive oil

1 tsp ground black pepper and 1 Tbsp salt,

1 tsp ground cinnamon,

1 tsp grated nutmeg,

1 tsp cumin powder,

1 tsp curry powder,

1 green chilli finely chopped

METHOD

Mix all ingredients and marinate for one hour. Insert into skewers and frill for 5 minutes on each side over hot coals. Serve with 'Jewels in Your Salad.'

INGREDIENTS - 'JEWELS IN YOUR SALAD'

A necklace of 22 baby carrots,

A necklace vine of glistening red baby tomatoes,

A gorgeous bouquet of 'Emerald' green lettuce leaves,

A string of sparkling baby 'Pearl' onions,

A generous sprinkle of 'Rubies' from fresh pomegranates,

Fresh herbs of parsley to garnish

These are the Jewels you will need to adorn the fresh country salad.

Drizzle with a salad dressing made from 'Amber Gold' honey, olive oil, salt and fresh lemon juice, it's a taste celebration for your tastebuds.

INGREDIENTS - SALAD DRESSING

1 Tbsp of 'golden' honey,

3 Tbsp of olive oil,

1 tsp salt,

Juice of 1 lemon,

Mix ingredients well and place in a bottle to drizzle over your 'Jewel Salad.'

METHOD

Carefully clean and rinse your Jewel vegetables, pat dry with a clean, dry dishcloth. In a large salad bowl break the bouquet of Emerald green leaves into individuals leaves and arrange them upright in a sparkling 'Crystal' salad bowl in a circle. Julienne* your necklace of 22 carrots to resemble 'matchsticks' remember you are creating a work of art, you are the 'Jeweller' creating this masterpiece of a salad that is going to impress the toughest food critic on Mother Earth. Place the julienne carrots in the centre of the sparkling 'Crystal bowl,' now place the glistening bright red baby tomatoes in the bowl and add in the baby 'Pearl' onions and toss these jewels slightly without disturbing the 'Emerald' green butter lettuce. At this point you do not drizzle salad dressing as it may cause the lettuce leaves to become soggy. It is best left to the individual to drizzle their own salad dressing. Last but not least, sprinkle generously with 'Rubies' from fresh pomegranates, to create your 'Masterpiece' of a Jewel Salad. Enjoy the taste sensation savouring your tastebuds. This salad can be served with fresh vegetables such as baked potatoes, zucchini or 'Gem' squash stuffed with buttery mixed vegetables.

Julienne vegetables cut into sticks resembling matchsticks.

HERITAGE

South Africa is a beautiful land of precious metals such as gold and silver and other metals, precious stones of world class diamonds. Gold was discovered in the interior of South Africa in the 1880's, railway lines had to be built to the ports creating economic development. South Africa is famous for its diamond industry. In 1867 the first diamond was discovered in the Kimberley region creating opportunities of business in South Africa and so the diamond rush was created bringing people to South Africa from all over the world. South African diamonds are famous for their size, quality and beauty.

ROOIBOS TEA

The story of rooibos teas and indigenous African tea is only found in the Cederberg area of the Western Cape where the climate is ideal for rooibos to grow. Traditional farming methods holds the secret to a delicious cup of rooibos tea. Hand harvested at dawn gives the tea a better taste. The arid wilderness and rocky terrain boast of crystal-clear streams of fresh water, this is the only place in the world where the rooibos tea bush grows. Rooibos tea has enormous health benefits. There are many medicinal properties to this rich mountain tea. On a hot summers day rooibos tea can be made into a thirst- quenching iced tea flavoured with slices of fresh fruit of your choice.

South Africa has many beautiful features ranging from the beautiful vineyards of the Western Cape to the snow-capped mountain of the Drakensberg in KwaZulu Natal and the majestic Table Mountain overlooking Robben Island where Nelson Mandela the symbol of democracy and South Africa's first black president was held prisoner.

PROTEAS - THE NATIONAL FLOWER OF SOUTH AFRICA

My story would not be complete if I did not write about our beautiful Protea flower. The majestic King Protea flower the symbol of the National Cricket Team of South Africa and is the national flower of South Africa. The protea flowers is indigenous to our country and adds beauty and splendour to our landscapes, it is a fynbos thus it does it is not a fussy plant and does not require much watering. It can grow in dry, arid regions.

Proteas are beautiful cut flowers to put in the vase and is an excellent export flower contributing to the economy of our country. I was pleasantly surprised to learn that proteas were grown for commercial purposes in KwaZulu Natal on a farm called 'Zulu Flora,' I came across this information on a YouTube channel called 'Farmer Proud.' The most popular protea grown on this farm is called the Yabba Sun. The climatic conditions make it ideal for these beauties to grow here as no irrigation is required. The rainfall in the region is sufficiently adequate for the flowers to bloom with ease.

The farms provide job opportunities for the local people, they are able to walk to work every morning and evening which is an advantage.

Our national bird is the Blue Crane, our national animal is the Springbok, the emblem for our national rugby team, 'The Springboks,' our national fish is the Galjoen, which is only found along the coasts of South Africa. It keeps mostly to the shallows which makes it ideal for the fishermen to catch.

Our country boasts of the beauty of the Namaqualand flowers which graces the landscapes of Namaqualand during the months of August and September. Special tour buses transport tourists to witness this spectacular flower display once a year and the flowers have never disappointed the viewer.

17

ANCESTRAL COMFORT FOODS

BUNNY CHOW
PROUDLY SOUTH AFRICAN INDIAN DISH

Bunny Chow

Bunny chow is basically a hollowed-out quarter of bread with a curry of your choice. One cannot eat a bunny chow with a fork and knife, the proper way to enjoy a bunny chow is to eat it using your fingers. Durban is a delightful place to dine when on holiday there, there are a variety of Indian restaurants to choose from to find the tasty bunny chow.

ORIGIN OF THE BUNNY CHOW

Bunny chow is derived from the word 'Bania' a term used for Indian immigrants. The restaurants selling food found that their bowls and plates went missing, to eradicate this problem the owner of the restaurant hollowed out loaves of bread and the bunny chow was born and is now a local cuisine. With such a rich diversity of culture and cuisine South Africa is a wonderful country of beautiful splendours ad awesome beauty.

INGREDIENTS - BUTTER BEANS CURRY

1 cup dried butter beans (soaked overnight)

1 litre water

1 onion sliced very fine

2 medium tomatoes grated

125ml cooking oil

1 sprig curry leaves

A few spring onion finely chopped

2 green chillies sliced in half

1 tsp ginger paste

1 tsp garlic paste

fresh coriander leaves to garnish

Potato may be added, it's optional

2 Tbsp masala and 1 tsp salt

1 tsp garam masala

1 tsp coriander powder

1 tsp cumin powder

1 tsp fennel powder

METHOD

Cook beans in the 1 litre of water and salt until it's soft and mushy. If you have a pressure pot that would be ideal. In a medium pot on medium heat add in oil to the pot. When the oil is slightly hot add in sliced onion and fry until it's translucent. Add in curry leaves, green chillies, and ginger and garlic paste and stir for 30 seconds. Add in spices stir and then add in the cooked beans, let this cook for 10 minutes before adding in grated tomatoes. Garnish with fresh coriander leaves and use as filling for your hollowed out bread to make a bunny chow or have it with rice and a carrot salad.

INGREDIENTS - CHICKEN CURRY FILLING

1 kg chicken portions

125ml cooking oil

1 onion sliced fine

2 tomatoes grated

1 sprig curry leaves

1 sprig thyme

2 green chillies sliced in half

2 tsp ginger paste

2 tsp garlic paste

Two medium potatoes quartered

2 tsp salt

Fresh coriander leaves to garnish

3 Tbsp masala

1 tsp garam masala

1 tsp fennel powder

1 tsp cumin powder

1 tsp coriander powder

2-star anise

1 cinnamon stick

3 cardamom pods

3 cloves (optional)

Be cautious when eating, be on the lookout for spices such as cardamom pods and cloves that may have landed in your plate. Do not eat these spices as they are very unpleasant to the taste buds but greatly enhance the flavour of food.

METHOD

Peel and quarter potatoes and place in a bowl of water to prevent oxidation. Grate 1 quarter of the potato and drizzle with a little oil to prevent discolouration, keep aside. In a pot on medium heat add in oil, when the oil is sufficiently hot add in sliced onion and fry until it's translucent, then add in curry leaves, sliced green chillies, ginger and garlic paste and stir for a few seconds thereafter add in spices and stir, add in tomatoes and cook for 1 minute. Add rinsed chicken and salt and stir well, do not add water at this stage, cook for fifteen minutes after which you add in the potatoes. When potatoes a half cooked check the consistency of the gravy, add little water at a time to make the gravy to your liking. Cook until potatoes are soft and garnish with fresh coriander.

TIP

Use 1 kg lamb using the same method to make lamb curry filling for bunny chow. Use 1 cup of mixed frozen or fresh vegetables such as diced carrots, green beans and peas to your bunny chow curry.

This delicious curry can be served with rice, savoury rice, rotis, or naan bread.

RECIPE FOR KITCHRI

Served with a tomato chutney on a cold, rainy day kitchri is a traditional favourite dish carried with pride from one generation to the next. Kitchri is an economical, tasty meal made from rice and dried split peas.

INGREDIENTS

1 cup rice

One and half tsp salt

Half a cup dried split pea

1 cup water

Quarter tsp asafoetida

Half a tsp turmeric powder

4 Tbsp oil

3 dried red chillies

1 onion, finely sliced

1 Tbsp ginger and garlic paste

1 cinnamon stick

2 cardamom pods

1 sprig curry leaves, removes leaves and rinse

1 tsp cumin seeds

1 tsp mustard seeds

Soak rice for an hour. Rinse dried split peas and add to a medium size pot, add in half a tsp of salt, quarter tsp asafoetida, asafoetida prevents flatulence, quarter tsp turmeric powder and a cup of water. Cook this until it's tender but not mushy. Keep aside.

METHOD

Braise onion until translucent, add in curry leaves, red chillies, cumin seeds, mustard seeds, cinnamon stick, turmeric and saute until onions turn golden in colour. Rinse rice well and add to braised onion mix, add in salt and a cup of water and stir well. Cook for half an hour, add in cooked split peas and cook further cook this until rice is tender. Serve with tomato chutney (Sauce.)

INGREDIENTS - TOMATO CHUTNEY (SAUCE)

4 medium ripe red tomatoes, preferably Roma tomatoes

1 onion thinly sliced

4 Tbsp oil

Quarter tsp turmeric powder

Half a tsp mustard seeds

Half a tsp cumin seeds

4 cloves garlic grated or blended

1 tsp salt

1 sprig curry leaves, rinsed and leaves removed

Half a cup of mint leaves rinsed

Half a cup of coriander leaves rinsed

METHOD

Grate or puree tomatoes, in a saucepan add oil and sauté onions on medium heat until it's translucent. Add chillies, curry leaves, mustard and cumin seeds, turmeric and garlic paste, cook this for a minute. Add in the turmeric powder and stir well. Add in tomato puree, salt and cook until the water has evaporated, add in the mint and coriander leaves and cook for a further two minutes, serve with kitchri.

TIP - VARIATION

For a variation add dry fish aka known as dry snoek or smoked haddock. Remember to boil salted dry fish well before adding to tomato chutney. Do not add salt to the tomato chutney if you are adding dry fish.

INGREDIENTS - DETOX KITCHRI

1 cup brown rice

Half a cup mung beans

1 cup water

2 tsp salt

Soak mung beans and brown rice for 3 hours prior to cooking. Rinse and cook with the 1 cup of water and 2 tsp salt. Cook thoroughly as undercooking causes flatulence.

4 Tbsp coconut oil

Half a cup cauliflower floret

Half a cup diced carrots

1 small onion finely sliced

1 tsp garam masala

Half a tsp turmeric powder

METHOD

Fry onion until golden brown, add in garam masala and turmeric powder and mix well. Add rinsed vegetables and steam until vegetables are cooked, add vegetables to kitchri and mix well.

DOSA RECIPE - PANCAKES

YVONNE SINGH'S HEARTWARMING SOUTH INDIAN DOSA WITH SPICY POTATO CURRY

The secret to making the perfect dosa is mixing all the ingredients correctly.

INGREDIENTS

1 cup all-purpose flour

Pinch of salt

2 cups of warm milk

3 Tbsp butter

3 eggs

METHOD

Make a well in the centre of the flour, add in 3 eggs and whisk, gradually add in the warm milk this way you won't get any lumps by gradually adding the milk. Whisk well, melt 3 Tbsp of butter and pour butter into dosa batter and continue stirring. Heat a non- stick pan to a moderate temperature, when hot enough pour a ladle full of dosa batter into pan. When the dosa is golden brown it is time to flip it. Flip and cook the other side until it's golden brown. Serve with spicy potato curry or a filling of your choice.

DOSA VARIATIONS

Add in 3 Tbsp sugar, 1 tsp vanilla essence to dosa batter, when it is cooked sprinkle with cinnamon powder and sugar. Can be eaten with a dollop of your favourite ice-cream.

INGREDIENTS - POTATO CURRY RECIPE

4 medium potatoes

1 large onion

2 green chillies

1 sprig curry leaves

1 tomato (optional)

120 ml oil

2 Tbsp masala

1 tsp turmeric powder

1 Tbsp salt

4 medium potatoes peeled and cut into wedges

1 large onion thinly sliced

2 green chillies sliced in half

1 sprig curry leaves rinsed and leaves removed

1 tomato (optional) 120 ml oil, 2 Tbsp masala

1 tsp turmeric powder

1 Tbsp salt

METHOD

In a medium pot on medium heat add oil, when the oil is fairly hot fry onions until golden brown. Set aside half of the onions. Add masala and turmeric powder and stir, add tomato and cook for 2 minutes, stir and add in potatoes, peas and salt, simmer for 1 minute before adding a cup of water, cook until the potatoes are soft. Once potatoes are cooked, add the fried onion that you set aside and stir well. Garnish with fresh coriander leaves. Serve with dosa or rice.

TIP

You can roast or air fry potatoes before making your curry to save on cooking time. Salt and toss potatoes in a Tbsp of oil and place on air fryer paper and fry in the air fryer or fry in a pan on the stove.

Famous Indian delights

A flashback into our history in the 1970's, 'Tamarind Hall of Fame.' You got to be old school to understand and appreciate our elders in this era. The old school vibes of disco music and everyone would be dancing like John Travolta in Saturday Night Fever and singing 'Night fever' to the tune of the Bee Gees, the anthem for the oldies. Men with long, sleek hair and women with straight long hair with a centre path, adorning themselves with the latest fashion and accessories. Bell bottom pants with wide bottoms which today is known as bootleg pants. Women at weddings with their vintage hairstyles, beautiful colourful sarees, jewellery and bright makeup and the men with their attire of suit and tie, sometimes the safari suit which the children would tease by calling it the 'suffering suit.' Today we emulate the vintage hairstyles then known as the 'gogo bun' an up-style bun made with curls that have been rolled up and sprayed with lots of hairspray.

Horsd'ouvres.[12] were served at a party. It was usually Vienna sausages cut into small pieces, cheese cut into blocks, cocktail tomatoes and cocktails onions inserted into a toothpick and then pierced into a pineapple with the crown still on. There was also a buffet table filled with platters of delicious snacks of chilli bites, spicy vedas.[13] samosas and other sweet treats. A large bowl of fruity punch made from fizzy granadilla cooldrink and grated apple would adorn the starter table.

I was still in primary school when Boney M a pop group from Jamaica sang 'By the Rivers of Babylon.' Boney M were popular and could be heard in almost every household in the neighbourhood, their songs were catchy and everyone would be singing to their songs. Today we still hear their song 'Mary's boy child' played at every mall a month before Christmas to get everyone into the mood of the Christmas season. Those are golden, Christmas memories. The legends would entertain us year after year during our Christmas lunch. A wonderful group with a wonderful combination of vocal talent. Listening to their Christmas songs made you feel warm inside, the festive season would not be complete without their soulful music.

Later in the nineties, functions would never be the same without 'that one aunt' who looked like a country cottage garden in her

---

[12] Horsd'oeuvres* starters or appetizers

[13] Vedas* spicy dried split pea fritters

floral dress and that 'one family member' who was 'the life of the party.' 'That one uncle' who could do the robot dance and breakdance on the dance floor to M.C Hammers, "Can't touch this." He was a crowd pleaser; it was uncle's gift to keep the guests entertained because they would all clap and cheer him on.

MEMORIES OF MY DAD

'Story time with my dad, childhood memories'

I am thankful for the significant impact my dad's bedtime stories had on me; it has created in me a love for reading. My dad would read to me phenomenal stories of Greek Mythology, the heroes of the land, the magnificence of the Greek world and their cultural history. I would listen attentively to these stories and these stories intrigued and fascinated me. My dad would always oblige to read me one more story even though he was sleepy and yawning constantly. Listening to the stories of ancient Greece created in me an appreciation and understanding of the land and I am looking forward to visiting there someday.

I am thankful for my dad's contribution to my love of storytelling, today I read bedtime stories to my grandchildren and nothing make me happier. I have inherited my dad's love for art and paintings as well, his favourite artist was Vincent van Gogh, two of his paintings (replicas) adorn the walls of my home. My dad's storytelling on the life of van Gogh would leave me feeling sad and emotional, he had a unique way of bringing stories to life. The tragic story of Vincent van Gogh cutting of his ear in a fit of rage and driven to insanity and despair was also the same man who had produced a masterpiece such as 'Starry Night.' There is a wonderful song sung about his tragic life called 'Vincent' by Don Maclean.

My dad would always buy us Cadbury chocolates especially the one with hazelnuts which was our favourite. I once asked him what were hazelnuts, his reply was 'its squirrels droppings?' I knew that he was joking and would laugh so hard that tears would roll down my cheeks. I loved his sense of humour. My gratitude to my humble, loving dad who is the absolute reason for me being an author today.

His warm eloquent voice, his gentle demeanour all made him a wonderful dad. Today I read of the planets, galaxies and dinosaurs to Zachary and 'the mouse who loved strawberries' to Zara which brings me great joy and fulfilment. I do read to Maila as well. There's never a dull moment being a grandma. May the world find true peace and beauty for our future generations. May we seek to instil the love of reading in them. May they pick up a book with eager anticipation and read it with pure joy. May their imaginations be enriched and create hours of reading pleasure.

Today I have chosen to live respectfully and live purposefully with ease and grace, to be blessing to society, today our society can also be found on the platforms of social media where we connect with the world. We find our long-lost friends here. For this I am thankful. As I reflect and embrace these stories and recipes which is a part of my culture and my heritage as a Proudly South African citizen, I am thankful to the citizen of Australia, Former South African Kelly Markey of Markey Writing Academy, my sponsor for her 'Power of Kindness' by paying it forward and making me write on an International Platform. My blessings and gratitude go to her.

May this book resonate with you the reader and may you be filled with nostalgic moments as turn the pages to remember the days of your youth, may this book radiate and pull at your heartstrings to remember your 'Momma' and the meals that she lovingly prepared for you whether it was simple or fancy. Love, light and gratitude to all.

My dad's favourite picture by Vincent van Gogh - Starry Night.

REFERENCE

Information on our Ancestors arriving from India was obtained from 1860 Heritage Centre. Facebook site.

Information on Honey - page 55 (Robin Jackson)

Information on Proteas - page 83 information obtained from YouTube Channel called 'Farmer Proud'

www.ingramcontent.com/pod-product-compliance
Lightning Source LLC
Chambersburg PA
CBHW062052290426
44109CB00027B/2798